Closing the equity gap

D0376037

Closing the equity gap

The impact of widening
participation strategies
in the UK and the USA

Edited by

Geoff Layer

Published by the National Institute of Adult Continuing Education
(England and Wales)
21 De Montfort Street, Leicester LE1 7GE
Company registration no: 2603322
Charity registration no: 1002775

First published 2005
© 2005 NIACE

NIACE has a broad remit to promote lifelong learning opportunities for adults.
NIACE works to develop increased participation in education and training,
particularly for those who do not have easy access because of barriers of class,
gender, age, race, language and culture, learning difficulties and disabilities, or
insufficient financial resources.

For a full catalogue of NIACE's publications, please visit

www.niace.org.uk/publications

Cataloguing in Publications Data
A CIP record for this title is available from the British Library

ISBN 1 86201 236 9

Cover design by Patrick Armstrong Book Production Services, London
Designed and typeset by Avon DataSet, Bidford-on-Avon, Warwickshire
Printed and bound in Great Britain by Antony Rowe

Contents

Contents

Acknowledgements

This book is a result of a seminar in March 2004, the views of the individuals who attended and the contributions of a range of authors. There are too many to thank individually but I would specifically like to thank Howard Newby and Chris Taylor for their encouragement, Jannette Cheong from HEFCE and Caroline Marston in Bradford for organising the seminar, David Longanecker from WICHE for securing the US participation, Rick Cryer for his dedicated proofreading, Virman Man from NIACE, the publisher, for careful tact and diplomacy over deadlines, all the seminar participants and my family for putting up with me.

Geoff Layer

Preface

This book represents a contribution to seeking to identify what has to be done to achieve greater social inclusivity within higher education. The book is based on work in both the United Kingdom and the United States of America in order to see how successful particular initiatives have been in changing the nature of higher education.

The book is based on the contributions to a bilateral seminar in Bradford at the end of March 2004 focussing on activities in the UK and the USA as part of an ongoing collaborative programme between the Higher Education Funding Council for England (HEFCE), Western Interstate Commission for Higher Education (WICHE) and State Higher Education Executive Officers (SHEEO). It was a time of change within both countries. The budget cuts in the USA were raising significant challenges about whether the existing level of commitment to equity programmes on education could be maintained. The level of budget reduction, in some cases 40%, determined that the existing strategy in the USA that had experienced some success would be difficult to support. This strategy tended to be a combination of student financial support and initiatives to encourage access. In the UK at the same time there was the major debate concerning the semi deregulation of tuition fees coupled with a drive to change the balance of who participated in higher education culminating in the Higher Education Act 2004.

The common aspect in both countries was the similarity of approach with a mixture of overall financial support together with a myriad of initiatives aimed at helping under represented groups into higher education but relatively little focus on what happened once they were in universities and colleges.

In both instances the approaches have failed to grasp the nettle of what needs to be done to achieve real change. It is important to ensure that students from all groups can afford to take up these higher education opportunities. However, the real change only takes place when the higher education 'offer' changes and reaches out to meet the needs of those who have traditionally been excluded. The challenge is to change the curriculum, the environment and the culture so that it meets the needs of the learners not to change the learner so that they meet the needs of the university.

The seminar re-inforced the need for a coherent strategy supported by institutional change. The danger is that we focus overly on who enters rather than looking at who can succeed.

© Tricia Malley and Ross Gillespie

Biography of Professor Colin Bell (1942–2003)

University successes in Professor Bell's period of office include radically overhauling the planning and budgeting procedures to increase transparency, effectiveness and efficiency and developing and agreeing the University's first-ever Corporate Plan. Under his leadership, the University achieved 'excellent' scores in five consecutive subject reviews and saw the opening of the prestigious new Graduate School.

He made a great impact at Bradford, and is remembered with warmth and respect by colleagues who felt that working with him meant that serious business was done but it was done in a spirit of enthusiasm, and often fun. One measure of his achievements is that he is remembered with appreciation for his professional contribution and affection for his personal qualities by those such as students and staff unions, who might conventionally be expected to be at loggerheads with Vice-Chancellors.

The University's reputation improved while he was at the helm. He coined the University's strapline 'confronting inequality: celebrating diversity', a phrase which he believed reflected the values of the University and one which he hoped would continue when he left.

Prior to his appointment at Bradford, he was Head of Edinburgh's Department of Sociology, before becoming Senior Vice-Principal with particular responsibilities for quality assurance, teaching, recruitment and student affairs. During his time there, he managed the 'merger' with Moray House Institute of Education.

He was a graduate, with first-class honours in History and Geography, of the University of Keele and the University of Wales, where he did postgraduate work at University College, Swansea, in Sociology and Social Anthropology.

He was appointed to a lectureship in the Sociology Department at the University of Essex in 1968 and was eventually Reader and Chair of that Department before taking up a Professorship of Sociology at the University of New South Wales in 1975. He was elected Chair of the Arts Faculty there. In 1980, he was appointed foundation Professor of Sociology at the University of Aston and Head of the Department of Sociology and Social History, from which he took voluntary redundancy in 1984.

After an appointment in research management in the University of Leicester Medical School he went to Edinburgh in 1986 and worked in educational evaluation in the Centre of Educational Sociology. He was appointed Professor of Sociology at Edinburgh in 1988. He has been a Visiting Professor at McMaster, Madison-Wisconsin and La Trobe.

He has been president of Section N (Sociology and Social Policy) of the British Association for the Advancement of Science and was elected a Fellow of the Royal Society of Edinburgh in 1990. He chaired the Scottish Higher Education Principals' (COSHEP) Quality Assurance Committee, as well as its Quality Assurance Forum. He was a member of the QAA's Degree Awarding Powers Committee. In 1999, he became one of the founding members of the Academy of Learned Societies for the Social Sciences.

Professor Bell was renowned for his fascination in far more than the academic and scholarly world. As well as being the author of a large number of scholarly papers on social mobility, family and marriage, stratification and power and research methodology, he has worked on agriculture, employment relationships, the environment and a wide variety of policy issues. His reading had spanned modern history, politics, philosophy, art, film and contemporary literature. He loved to travel and to entertain and remained a lifelong Ipswich supporter. His enthusiasm for, and knowledge of, jazz and blues was legendary.

After graduating from Keele, Professor Bell married Jocelyn Mumford and became a father to Rachel and Luke. In 1987, he married Dr Jan Webb with whom he had two children, Islay and Catherine.

"In his three years at the University he completely revolutionised the structure of departments, which to this day is still in place. He had a good understanding of the things that make universities tick".

University Senior Pro-Chancellor and Chairperson
of Council, Tommy Ashdown

"Colin Bell was at Bradford for only three years but in that time he stamped his own distinctive mark on the University. His managerial style was empowering, inclusive and persuasive, but nevertheless he was both decisive and courageous when necessary. His personality was different from previous Vice-Chancellors and he took advantage of this to push through the changes he thought necessary."

Chancellor of the University, Baroness Lockwood

"Colin Bell was an inspirational teacher, researcher and academic leader, especially in the social sciences. But he was much more than this. For Colin, life was a campaign of social justice and his chosen profession a means of achieving a more humane and enlightened society. His commitment to make the world a better place was personal as well as public."

Chief Executive of the Higher Education Funding
Council for England, Sir Howard Newby

"He was always excellent company and was as adept in his recommendation of good films as he was eloquent about the latest jazz

CDs. Life was there to be grasped rather than simply contemplated, and he knew when to press his own rationally and empirically informed opinions. His contribution to the university and society has been sadly cut short."

Former Principal of Edinburgh University, Lord Sutherland

The Colin Bell Memorial Lecture

Doing widening participation: social inequality and access to higher education

30 March 2004

Howard Newby

I am sure that many of you will understand the sense of privilege and responsibility that I have this evening in delivering the Colin Bell Memorial Lecture. Colin was my mentor, colleague and friend for over 35 years and his sudden death last year was a terrible blow to his family, friends and colleagues everywhere. As Colin was fond of saying to some of our slightly bemused Vice-Chancellor colleagues, he and I 'have a past'. We first came together in 1968 when he was my undergraduate tutor. He later became my Ph.D. supervisor, co-author and lifelong friend. One of the books we edited together was entitled *Doing Sociological Research* (Bell and Newby, 1977), a collection of essays in which the authors of classic sociological studies from the 1960s and 1970s owned up about what it was really like to undertake research as opposed to those rather airbrushed accounts one usually finds in the second chapter of a book or thesis. The first part of the title of this lecture is therefore an allusion to the collaboration between Colin and myself but the second half of the title refers to an issue on which Colin felt so strongly during his lifetime as an academic. So in this lecture I want to address a number of key issues about social inequality and access to higher education. This is, of course, seen through the distorting lens of someone who has, as a participant, observed higher education policy on widening participation over the last two and a half years in my present role as Chief Executive of the Higher Education Funding Council for England (HEFCE).

You can perhaps understand the sense of obligation I feel to Colin's memory in tackling this topic. In my speech at Colin's funeral in Stirling last year I referred to two of the abiding themes of Colin's professional career. He had an immense fascination with epistemology – in other words the issue of how we know what we know. What counted as evidence and how we interpreted it was something that never ceased to fascinate him. It was this issue, above all else, that enabled Colin to inspire a whole generation of graduate students who came under his spell. Colin's restless mind and boundless curiosity never failed to ignite a response among those who worked with him and for him, myself included.

Colin's other great passion was for social justice. He believed passionately in equality of opportunity. He thrived on assisting individual students to achieve their potential and he was intolerant of arguments, no matter how well disguised, which seek to veil the defence of privilege with a pretence of apparently disinterested intellectual discourse. Despite Colin's deeply held scepticism about the nature of evidence, he never failed to seek out the empirical support for proposals which would promote equality of opportunity. Colin's sociological practice was always what we would now call 'evidence-based'. He was an empirical sociologist, even though he abhorred empiricism; but he was always the kind of sociologist who, to use C. Wright Mills's famous distinction, sought to link private troubles with public issues.

This is particularly apparent in Colin's approach to the study of what we would now call 'life-chances'. Sociologists among you will know that the concept originally comes from the work of Max Weber. In its most precise form the notion of life-chances can be expressed as a set of statistical probabilities: what are, literally, the chances of an individual being born into one class or status group achieving over their lifetime mobility into another? Indeed this very approach to life-chances is used by modern researchers into social mobility. Very early on Colin cottoned on to the fact that an individual's life-chances could be immensely increased by access to education, including higher education. This was very apparent in his first major work, *Middle-Class Families* (Bell 1968), based upon his Master's thesis at University College, Swansea. Colin recognised that education had been a major driver of social mobility among those middle-class families whom he interviewed. The geographer, which often lurked just beneath the sociologist in Colin's mind, also recognised that this was frequently linked to geographical mobililty – in other words, in order to move up the social scale individuals often had to move geographically from one part of the country to another as they pursued their upwardly mobile careers. Education, social mobility and equality of opportunity were therefore intimately linked in Colin's approach to social justice.

He was also influenced in this by the work of several educational sociologists in the early 1960s; most notably Brian Jackson and Dennis Marsden's book *Education and the Working Class* (1966). This demonstrated that the local community (especially through peer group pressure), family structure and educational opportunity were defining ingredients in helping or hindering the progress of that 1950s cliché, the working-class grammar school child. Not the least of the frustrations I feel at the present time is that we probably know less today than we did then about how family, community, school experience and social sub-cultures intersect to help or hinder both the aspirations and achievements of children from backgrounds who have not traditionally participated in higher education. So instead recent public debate has proceeded by assertions which are scarcely grounded in serious empirical evidence. On the one hand we have elaborations with varying degrees of sophistication of the 'more means worse' argument. On the other hand we have a somewhat simplistic assumption that higher education is a panacea for solving all the social and economic ills of the modern age. The result is all too often – as I know personally – the development and implementation of policy on widening access to higher education ahead of appropriate research evidence.

By now you will have discerned some of the themes that I wish to take up in this lecture. I want to reassert why widening participation in higher education matters. I want to do this not from an ideological standpoint, although I happen to be ideologically committed to just such a view, but also from a purely rational and utilitarian standpoint, since this approach to higher education has, rather depressingly, been prevalent in recent years and higher education has been seen as the means to an end, usually a means of achieving global competitiveness in an increasingly knowledge-based economy. But I do want to reassert that in a higher education environment that can at times seem dominated by the tensions of under-funding, under-planning and the prospective impact of variable fees serving to stimulate a market, we should not lose sight of our commitment to increasing and widening participation in higher education and thereby improve the life-chances of all of our citizens.

The need to underline this commitment may seem to many people in this audience as curious. After all we have a government in power which was elected on the basis of a manifesto commitment that 50 per cent of 18–30-year-olds should have some experience of higher education by 2010. This election manifesto commitment has also been translated into the more mundane currency of a PSA target set by the Treasury for the Department for Education and Skills (DfES). This is, indeed, a far-reaching commitment. It is statistically highly unlikely that we could achieve a 50 per cent participation rate in higher education without simultaneously widening it. In other words to achieve such a high rate of participation in higher education we also need to improve the social mix of our students. So the 50 per cent target is not just about the arithmetic of student places. It is also about extending educational opportunity to those who have not traditionally aspired to, nor, in terms of their education attainment, achieved entry into a higher education institution. The broad parameters of this problem are by now well known. With one or two exceptions, such as Bangladeshi females and Afro-Caribbean males, most ethnic minority groups are well represented – indeed over-represented – in higher education in England, although their distribution varies enormously between institutions. Similarly, females are over-represented and the sector has a defensible record on catering for students with disabilities. The last frontier of participation in higher education, however, refers to the social class mix. As is well known, while overall participation in higher education has moved from one in seven to just under one in two over the last 15 years, the gap in participation rates between the top and bottom socio-economic classes has moved only slightly. The issue therefore is how to extend opportunity to participate in higher education to young people from family backgrounds in what the Office of National Statistics would call social classes C2, D and E – essentially semi-skilled and unskilled manual occupations. No matter which way you look at it, their life-chances, in terms of their ability to access higher education and thereby access graduate-level jobs, remain severely restricted.

I have already alluded to the fact that one could look at this issue ideologically. I am sure that if Colin were here he would be committed to the 50 per cent target purely in terms of social justice and equality of opportunity. Many commentators have, indeed, accused the present government of being purely ideologically motivated in its commitment to the 50 per cent target. Phrases abound about the target having been 'plucked from thin air' or been purely arrived at through political dogma. Anyone who has participated in successive government spending reviews would find this hard to believe. Whatever the nature of the manifesto commitment the Treasury has its own means of establishing the desirability of spending billions of pounds of public money. The 50 per cent target would not survive one nano-second of the Treasury's gimlet-eyed analysis of value for money over public spending priorities. So there must be more to it than this. What can this possibly be?

While I would not wish to underestimate the political commitment to widening participation in higher education, the main driver is much more rational and utilitarian. It is based upon the recognition that, inevitably, the UK is moving, and will move, towards an economy whose sustainability will depend very much more on the skills of its human resources. The phrase 'knowledge based economy' may be a cliché, but at its heart lies the accurate perception that in the long-term the UK's only comparative advantage, if it is to compete successfully in the global economy, is its people. So the origins of the 50 per cent target lie in studies conducted in the late 1990s which established – whether accurately or otherwise remains to be seen – that the majority of new jobs created over the first decade of the twenty-first century would be those which would require graduate-level skills – about 70 per cent of them. From then on it is a matter of simple arithmetic to turn this into a sustainable number of graduates which the higher education system needs to produce every year and from this it is easy to wind it back into a participation rate in higher education. This was how the 50 per cent target came about. Now one can have an argument about whether or not these forecasts are accurate and whether or not the kind of skills which graduates have are those which are going to be in greater demand by the end of this decade. There is indeed some short-term evidence that high-skill occupations have a low percentage share of the total unfilled vacancies in comparison to intermediate and low-skill occupations in the last couple of years. But one can also point to the fact that the huge expansion in graduate numbers over the last decade has not reduced the premium in lifetime earnings for those who have degrees. It does seem to be the case that the market is capable of absorbing a far greater number of graduates than was the case less than a generation ago.

But even if we don't need graduates to fill a skills gap, do we need them to increase productivity and stimulate economic growth? The answer to this question in the affirmative underpins many of the policies that propose an increased investment in higher education. But no one, *pace* Alison Wolf (2002), suggests that increased investment in higher education *alone* is necessary to improve productivity. So Alison Wolf attacks a rather easy target – what would be called in less politically correct times, a straw man. Certainly there is evidence of a positive correlation between higher education expenditure and per capita income growth but no clear evidence of a causal relationship between the two. It is indeed extremely difficult to prove any causal link between higher education and productivity as it is impossible to know whether a graduate is more productive simply by virtue of being a graduate. In addition, any analysis relies on formal qualifications and wages as measures: this is problematic as qualifications cannot take account of skills, and wages reflect a lot more than simply productivity. So it may or may not be the case that we need graduates to increase productivity and stimulate economic growth. The evidence is either not there or simply confusing.

However, one of the most frequently quoted and perhaps most compelling reasons for widening participation, is the increased private rate of return to graduates. It has been calculated that men and women with higher education qualifications have a 15 per cent and 20 per cent wage premium respectively over men and women without a first degree. We have also heard that graduates earn on average £400,000 more in their working lives than non-graduates. We also know, however, that it is extremely difficult to calculate the graduate premium received just by virtue of being a graduate as the control group of non-graduates simply does not exist anymore as nearly all students who achieve two or more A-levels now go on to higher education study. Despite these difficulties, though, the rate of return still remains a strong driver in the decision to enter higher education; although the premium may or may not be £400,000 it is still considered to be very large and significant.

There is also an element of self-fulfilling prophecy about all this, because of the expectation among young people that as more of them graduate with degrees so access to the best jobs will be limited without one. Therefore, the higher the participation rate the more rational is the choice to participate in higher education. The Higher Education Policy Institute (HEPI, 2003) has recently cited evidence from the USA, where participation is already over 50 per cent, which shows that not only has there been an increase in wage inequality but there has also been a decline in real terms of the earnings of the lowest tenth percentile. This alone should be reason enough to ensure that access to higher education in the UK is not just passively made available to all who can benefit from it but is actively promoted and made an achievable reality to under-represented groups.

The evidence that there is a high rate of private return for graduates is a fact which, of course, underlies the government's recent proposals that students should pay a higher percentage of the cost of their higher education over their lifetime. It also reflects the fact that as we move to a more knowledge-based economy so participation in higher education will underpin social inclusiveness. As the participation rate increases those who have not participated in higher education will increasingly feel – and possibly will be – more socially excluded. It is this combination of higher education being both a public and a private good which makes the current debates about the future of higher education policy so contestable.

Indeed these difficulties are compounded when the private rate of return for graduates is placed in the broader context. As Brynner et al. (2003) have commented:

> 'Apart from the returns in terms of increased earnings, consumption patterns and lifestyle that graduates enjoy, graduates also cost the community less. They are less likely to require social security benefits to see them through periods of unemployment. Their generally higher levels of health and a healthier lifestyle means they are less of a burden on the NHS. They also contribute to social cohesion through the values they hold and the voluntary and community activity that they undertake. They provide these benefits not only directly but also indirectly through the transmission of their own educational capital to their children. This inter-generational transfer helps to ensure that the next generation will not only enjoy the HE benefits personally but will also contribute to the well being of society as a whole'.

Bynner et al. (2003) admit that they cannot claim that graduating from higher education is the prerequisite for the accumulation of social capital, but they do show that graduates are the most likely to manifest these qualities.

And here we need to remind ourselves that higher education is more than a means to an end. Although there are arguments which can be mounted in terms of the economic benefits of mass higher education, we should not overlook our commitment to the wider social and cultural benefits which can also accrue. Higher education institutions are an important element of civil society. They are institutions which stand between the State and the individual, mediating relationships between the two. In an increasingly secular society this is a not in-considerable factor. Universities are repositories of culture, learning and civilising values. Indeed the Catalan sociologist, Manuel Castells

(2000), has argued that universities are a core element in inculcating civilising values in a multi-ethnic and multi-faith world. It has not been fashionable recently to reassert the values of the European Enlightenment, but I would suggest that the vast majority of those involved in higher education are committed to the notion that the growth of knowledge is the major driver of social progress. Therefore, there is more to higher education than a core function of contributing to economic growth. The defence of reason, the cultivation of young minds, and the extension of a civilising influence are not the kind of concepts which pass the test of Treasury scrutiny in spending reviews. Nevertheless that is no reason why we in the higher education world should abandon them and whilst the present Secretary of State was quite right to point out that a medieval concept of a university can only be supported by medieval funding levels, we should not forget either what it is that makes higher education higher. In every sense.

It is one thing to recognise the economic, social, and indeed, moral force of the argument to favour a mass higher education system in this country. It is quite another to implement it. We have, after all, been here before. With the creation of the polytechnic sector in the late 1960s, access to higher education increased significantly. The remit from the Council for National Academic Awards was to extend access to a much wider range of students, and the polytechnics expanded at a much faster rate than predicted or planned. Most polytechnics admitted mature students after the age of 21 without the traditional entry qualifications of two or more A-levels and they devised access courses, part-time courses, recognised experiential and prior learning, etc. and so significantly advanced the cause of widening participation long before it became a political imperative. This, of course, remains true today, although it has been argued by some commentators that there has been a growing academic convergence between the pre-1992 and post-1992 universities. In other words it has been argued that since their early development the polytechnics, as they then were, had developed programmes that have become increasingly 'academic' and similar to those offered in the former university sector, just as the pre-1992 universities have developed courses which have become increasingly vocational and labour market-oriented. I shall return to this issue in a moment. In the meantime it has perhaps not been surprising, as Archer et al. (2003) have recently suggested, that for all the expansion of the 1990s there has been a persistent, consistent and continuing tendency to recruit students from the middle classes. As they point out:

> 'The size of the middle class has itself increased but this is a relatively minor explanatory factor. Over the same period, it has become acknowledged that the possession of a higher education qualification confers powers and privileges. Graduates are differentially incorporated into civil society and benefit materially in status'.

Thus both the demand and the supply of higher education places has risen almost hand-in-hand over the last decade or more. In absolute terms more young people from poorer backgrounds have entered into, and graduated from, higher education institutions. But the proportions have only very slightly changed. Why might this be? One possible explanation might be that universities and colleges are somehow systematically discriminating against candidates from poorer backgrounds through their admissions processes. The case of Laura Spence, the applicant from a Tyneside comprehensive school who was turned down for a place at an Oxford college three years ago, became a national *cause celebre* about the alleged lack of transparency and accountability of university admissions processes. However, there is no evidence of a systematic social bias in university admissions, as a National Audit Office Report on widening participation concluded in 2002 (NAO 2002a). Perceptions might, of course, be different and the group under the chairmanship of Professor Stephen Schwartz, Vice-Chancellor of Brunel University, will shortly propose guidance on admissions procedures in a bid to restore wider public confidence in the sector's practices.

This having been said, the empirical evidence is that proportionately fewer young people from poor backgrounds enter higher education because fewer of them present themselves, rather than because admissions procedures are necessarily biased against them. And there are at least two plausible sets of reasons as to why this might be the case. The first is that demand is lacking because of a lack of achievement in those schools and colleges in which poor schoolchildren are disproportionately clustered and that there might also be a failure of aspiration even to consider higher education as a feasible and desirable opportunity.

We know that prior educational attainment is the major determining factor in participation in higher education. We also know that post-16 staying-on rates for the lower socio-economic groups are low especially in comparison with our major economic competitors. In the higher education sector we often find ourselves at the end of a supply chain from schools and colleges over which we have very little control, a situation, I cannot resist remarking, which would not be tolerated in the private sector. The question is what can we, as a higher education sector, do about it?

The sector has already recognised that to make any real difference we need to reach out into schools and colleges and, in the spirit of partnership, work with them to raise aspirations and to improve achievement. This is the philosophy which lies behind Partnerships for Progression, the HEFCE and Learning and Skills Council programme which has now been absorbed into Aimhigher. Many higher education institutions have student mentors going into schools to share their experiences of, and knowledge about, higher education with young people who would ordinarily not consider entry into higher education as an option. We also know that parents have a great influence on whether or not their offspring consider higher education as a serious option so work needs to be done to educate parents and engage them with the idea of higher education. Teachers and guidance counsellors also need to be made fully aware of the routes into and through higher education so that they can offer the best advice to their pupils. All too often it is those who require the most information who have access to the least. Such measures are by no means comprehensive and much more needs to be done. For our part at the Funding Council we have increased very substantially the resources available to both recruit and retain students from non-traditional backgrounds. We recognise the increased costs in engaging in such activity and we wish to do what we can to support and to encourage it. But I would be the first to admit that we still do not know, in any definitive way, what works. This is where the lack of pertinent research evidence is so frustrating.

I am probably not alone, however, in believing that these demand-led interventions are not in themselves going to be sufficient, valuable though they are. This is why, in the remainder of this lecture, I want to focus on a second set of issues; those concerned with the supply side.

As we move from an elite to a more mass higher education system it is unreasonable to believe that we will succeed simply by offering 'more of the same'. If the rationale of higher participation is the need of the economy for a greater volume of graduate-level skills, then it is incumbent upon the sector to ensure that these skills and competence are fit for purpose in the modern world. Graduates, too, expect their skills to be more attuned to the needs of the labour market. This is not to argue that higher education becomes somehow merged with the much narrower concept of training, but it does suggest that higher education will encompass a wider range of both academic and vocational programmes than was the case when universities supplied graduates to just a few elite professions.

This issue presents the sector with a number of challenges. On this analysis higher education should become more ubiquitous, yet there remain parts of the country where provision remains lacking or under-represented. Moreover, as higher education moves from being a 'once-in-a-lifetime' opportunity to a lifelong requirement which needs to be refreshed and updated across a lifetime, so it needs to be delivered in a more flexible, student-centred form – part-time, as well as full-time, in the workplace, on-line, via distance learning, and so forth. Despite much progress over the last decade in recognising the importance of lifelong learning, we are still some way from following through the implications. Widening participation will mean more than just persuading a greater proportion of non-traditional students to apply to university; it will also mean adapting the content and delivery of higher education to make it more relevant to their needs.

Let me be clear here. I am not suggesting that standards need to be lowered to accommodate more non-traditional students. That would, indeed, be a betrayal to the students themselves and would be in any case (as I shall outline in a moment) unnecessary. What I am referring to here is the need to ensure that higher education accommodates the 'vocational' as well as the 'academic' in the same way that, from the nineteenth century onwards it encompassed the vocational needs of lawyers, doctors, engineers and so on. A purely 'academic' form of higher education will not suffice, even if we recognise that what we now call 'academic' degree programmes have always had embedded within them the acquisition of appropriate 'vocational' skills.

As the Tomlinson report on 14–19 education (Tomlinson, 2003) has recently recognised, this distinction between 'academic' and 'vocational' types of education is become increasingly outmoded. Yet it continues to bedevil post-compulsory education. The sociologist in me suspects that lurking beneath the surface here is a typically English concern for status, expressed in a binary distinction which does not withstand critical scrutiny. Even within some parts of higher education the understanding of how the 'vocational' and the 'academic' aspects of learning relate to each other seems fairly rudimentary. Compare this with our more sophisticated understanding of research. Today we recognise that terms like 'basic' and 'applied' research are increasingly outmoded. We also recognise that research is a spectrum of activity incorporating the creative elements of knowledge and understanding, but also what we now call knowledge transfer – the ways in which we seek to ensure that this knowledge is made available to all users who might benefit from it. Now apply this by analogy to learning and teaching: we not only need to ensure our students acquire new knowledge and understanding, but also that they understand how this relates to *using* it. The academic and the vocational are not a distinction, but a spectrum. And how much better would our knowledge transfer activity be if the academic *and* the vocational were integrated in our learning and teaching.

How far away we remain from this can easily be illustrated by the current pattern of post-16 education England. At present while there is now a very clear post-16 educational pathway for those who choose the more academic route of A-levels and direct university entrance, there still remains immense confusion around the post-16 pathway for those students wishing to take a more vocational route. For the 16-year-old who wishes to go to university the message is clear: obtain two A-levels and you will find a place. It may not be a place in the university of your choice but one will be available for you somewhere. For the 16-year-old who wishes to follow a more vocational route what then is the message? It is perhaps to follow a B.Tec qualification, an HNC or HND, perhaps these days to move on to a Foundation Degree and, with luck, and by the grace of an admissions tutor, to top this up with an Honours Degree. Or it might mean vocational A-levels, an advanced modern apprenticeship, a foundation year in a further education (FE) college and then, again, if you are lucky and by the grace and favour of an admissions tutor, admission to a university. The vocational pathway is neither clear nor consistently applied. It varies enormously from one part of the country to another and it is therefore simply not clear to a 16-year-old what this pathway is and where it will lead. This is a travesty of modern higher education which would scarcely be tolerated by any of our major industrial competitors. If we are to develop a genuine mass higher education system then pathways into and through higher education should be clear to any student at any point of entry. This is the very best aspect of much of the American higher education experience, particularly in those public university systems which have been adopted by the most progressive American states. I do not need to remind this audience that higher education sits within the context of lifelong learning and yet we still do not have the progression routes, the pathways or even the credit transfer systems which would allow a genuine system of lifelong learning to be developed and marketed to those who might need it most.

All of this results in a high disparity in post-16 progression. About 90 per cent of those on conventional A-level programmes enter higher education, but only 40 to 50 per cent of those qualifying at level 3 in vocational subjects do so. I doubt very much whether these statistics will be radically changed simply by examining universities' and colleges' admissions procedures. The core of any progression strategy will be the ability of learners to move between different programmes and, if necessary, institutions in order to fulfil their potential. In the United States, for example, institutions with distinctly different missions have a common interest in ensuring such opportunities are available, and in putting arrangements in place to facilitate it. All educational institutions are committed to ensuring that anyone with the ability to benefit from higher education has access to the programmes that meet their needs and abilities. The prospects opened up by improved arrangements for progression have attracted more students to higher education (HE), and have encouraged many more to return to learning over a working lifetime.

Here in the UK we have not developed higher education in the planned way that characterises the American public university systems. Moreover, in England the sheer size and scale of post-16 provision probably rules out for the foreseeable future the kinds of tertiary arrangements which are being taken forward in Scotland and Wales. Nevertheless, we may have to look again at certain other aspects of how further education relates to higher education, not least because Scotland has demonstrated just how important this link is to both raising and widening participation.

We certainly need to recognise the enhanced role of further education colleges in providing the necessary progression routes post-16. But we also need to recognise that, as presently constituted, most further education colleges have an enormous span of activity – from basic numeracy and literacy skills to higher education. I sometimes wonder whether this amounts to a mission stretch which goes too far. Should we not be looking at how we can develop a group of institutions in the FE sector specifically focused on delivering post-16 students from under-represented backgrounds to higher education? This would certainly be one step towards improving the attractiveness, consistency and marketability of vocational higher education in particular and in this I welcome Foundation Degrees as a step in the right direction. However, we are still a long way from the best of the North American systems where a student can enter any institution within an overall state university system and proceed, if necessary, to a Ph.D. in some of the best research universities in the world. There are clear progression routes, workable credit accumulation and transfer systems and a general sense that the best interests of the most research-intensive universities are well served by spreading the social base of higher education as widely as possible. All too often in this country, alas, the reverse is true – the spread of higher education is somehow seen as a threat to our research-intensive universities.

I simply do not see why this has to be. The Funding Council does not, of course, have planning powers and here lies the rub. Nobody does. So while everyone recognises the importance of lifelong learning, educational progression, widening participation and flexibility of delivery, institutional and sectional interests often get in the way. At a time when it is imperative that institutions 'play to their strengths', leading to the emergence of a more diverse sector, so it will become even more important that the whole range of educational opportunity is available to learners as their lifetime needs, interests and abilities develop. It is likely, therefore, that at the Funding Council we will need to pay greater attention to how we can encourage institutions, both FE and HE, to connect to each other, creating the sense of seamless progression along clearly signposted pathways which characterises the best of American public university practice.

This is not a euphemism for proposing wholesale mergers. Rather, it is an attempt to create networks of institutions – what we have called Lifelong Learning Networks – which would typically link colleges and Higher Education Institutions (HEIs) across a city, region or area that potential learners can identify with. Such networks would:

- combine the strengths of a number of diverse institutions;
- provide support for learners on vocational pathways;
- bring greater clarity, coherence and certainty to progression opportunities;
- develop the curriculum as appropriate to facilitate progression;
- value vocational learning outcomes and provide opportunities for vocational learners to build on earlier learning;
- locate the progression strategy within a commitment to lifelong learning, ensuring that learners have access to a range of progression opportunities such that they can move between different kinds of vocational-academic programmes as their interests, needs and abilities develop.

Lifelong Learning Networks would therefore offer a wide-ranging curriculum, combining the strengths of further and higher education. They would include colleges that are centres of vocational excellence and those with significant higher education provision of their own: HEIs with a research-intensive mission as well as those more focused on teaching and engaged in serving local and regional economies. At the heart of every Network will be arrangements to facilitate progression. A Network would, for example, offer a guarantee to learners that they will be able to progress from any award offered by one of the partners to any other programme offered within the Network that the learner is adequately prepared for, and can benefit from. This does not mean, however, that every Network would be the same. They would be designed to meet specific needs and developed through a process of consultation and business planning.

Lifelong Learning Networks would therefore maximise opportunities in the local and regional context. We would expect each of the Networks to link with the regional arm of the Sector Skills Councils most closely associated with the employment clusters central to the economic life or future of the region, and to other regional bodies such as regional development agencies. Networks would also contribute more generally to local economic and labour market planning to meet the training, economic development and regeneration needs of regions through research and links with business. Similarly, such Networks would build on the work of Centres of Vocational Excellence (CoVEs) in colleges, and Centres for Excellence in Teaching and Learning (CETLs) in HEIs, linking also with New Technology Institutes and new Knowledge Exchanges as these are established. But lifelong learning for the individual should not be confined to the tracks or pathways indicated by the starting point. Research-intensive institutions will bring their own strengths to the partnership and it will be crucial to establish ways to facilitate this.

We do not expect every Network to develop all of these links or to accord the same priority to each of the links that are established. The first Networks will be pilots, 'demonstrators' that test what works and develop models capable of being generalised. The initial focus for the Network might therefore be any one (or more) of the many focal points and links available to them. What they will have in common is the aim of improving progression opportunities. In this they will add value to what institutions already do because they will extend the reach of initiatives developed in one or more institutions to all the participants in the area covered by the Network. For example, institutions across the Network could consider what they can add to the work of CoVEs by offering progression routes to a wide range of existing programmes and collaboration on the curriculum development required to provide opportunities that do not already exist. Flourishing links with the local economy through Knowledge Exchanges can feed back into the curriculum; the curriculum offered in CETLs might have a core role in a Network, seeking to overcome differences in learning and teaching styles that too often limit progression. Above all, the Network would add value because it is learner-centred, and learner-driven, but on a scale, and with a variety of provision, that no single provider can offer.

I am very aware that something akin to Lifelong Learning Networks – at least in embryonic form – are in existence in certain parts of the country already. So what I am proposing here is an extension of best practice in a more formalised form which runs with the grain of much existing local and regional thinking. A wholesale restructuring of post-16 education is not a feasible proposition, even if it might be desirable. So we must strive to achieve a more evolutionary approach, but one which structures provision around the needs of the learners rather than takes existing institutional relationships as immutable. More diversity in higher education must be accompanied by not only more collaboration, but more connectivity, if we are to move towards 50 per cent participation and seriously address fair access.

As I hinted earlier in this lecture, there will be some who say that all of this will mean lowering standards in higher education. I reject this argument completely. In order to achieve a mass higher education system in this country there is absolutely no need to lower standards. Rather we need to extend to that as yet untapped pool of talent in the lower socioeconomic groups the same opportunities that are already extended to those in social classes A, B and C1. There is an enormous pool of talent on which to draw if only it can be extended and nurtured in the same way that the talents already in higher education have been over the last generation. It would be a betrayal to lower standards in any case. There is no sense in extending to non-traditional students a false prospectus, a secondary modern version of higher education which betrays their aspirations and is of doubtful value for money to the nation as a whole. The evidence of the last 20 years is that more does not mean worse. UK higher education has expanded exponentially and has been transformed to the benefit of all who have participated in it. Ah, but some might say, don't we need more plumbers rather than more graduates. I find this argument fascinating. It seems to reflect a certain degree of middle class angst against paying an hourly rate to plumbers that might approximate to the hourly rate paid to solicitors and other professionals. But even if we accept that in our centrally heated homes we need more plumbers and heating engineers, surely it should not be a choice between educating more plumbers and educating more graduates. The truth of the matter is that we need both. And yes, much needs to be done about the level of technical education in this country. All this talk about plumbers and graduates smacks of a very English concern with people being 'too clever by half', a phrase which would be almost incomprehensible in any other country. Education should not be a positional good in which more for some means less for others. Education is a public investment, a private good and a human right.

Colin would have understood these sentiments and spent his time as Vice-Chancellor both here in Bradford and in Stirling in leading the higher education sector towards a recognition of that goal. He, more than anyone, would have recognised the political dimension of widening participation and fair access and have fought to ensure that the political will was there to expand higher education in a more socially inclusive way. Like Colin, I believe passionately that we have some way to travel if we are to achieve systemic change in educational progression. We need to work harder on joined-up policy to ensure that we have in place clear pathways of progression for students whether from the traditional academic routes or from vocational routes to higher education. In the era of lifelong learning we need to be able to offer and deliver what might be described as a systemic approach to higher education: progression routes that offer to all students the opportunity to move in and out of higher education throughout their working lives.

Higher education is a major force in our civil society. We need to engage with ideas and opportunities that will deliver the *future* as opposed to funding approaches and delivery mechanisms that delivered the *past*. We are here to honour the life of a colleague, thinker, and reformer who believed passionately that higher education was a force for social improvement. It is fitting and proper that we should meet at Bradford University to honour the commitment of Colin Bell to widening participation. We have a duty to dedicate ourselves to the work unfinished by Colin. This is a task as daunting as it is inspiring. We should settle for nothing less.

References

Archer, L., Hutchings, M. and Ross, A. (2003) *Higher Education and Social Class: Issues of Exclusion and Inclusion.* London: Routledge Falmer.

Aston, L. and Bekhradnia, B. (2003) *Demand for graduates: a review of the economic evidence.* Oxford: Higher Education Policy Institute (HEPI).

Aston, L. (2003) *Higher education supply and demand to 2010.* Oxford: Higher Education Policy Institute (HEPI).

Bell, C. (1968) *Middle Class Families: Social and Geographical Mobility.* London: Routledge and Kegan Paul.

Bell, C. and Newby, H. (1977) *Doing Sociological Research.* London: Allen and Unwin.

Bynner, J. et al. (2003) *Revisiting the benefits of Higher Education.* Bristol: HEFCE.

Castells, M. (2000) *The Rise Of The Network Society.* Oxford: Blackwell.

Connor, H., Tyers, C., Modood, T. and Hillage, J. (2004) *Why the difference? A Closer look at Higher Education Minority Ethnic Students and Graduates*, Research Report RR552. Sheffield: DfES.

Higher Education Funding Council for England (HEFCE) *Supply and demand in higher education.* HEFCE 01/62, Bristol: HEFCE.

HEFCE *Funding for widening participation in higher education.* HEFCE 2003/14.

HEFCE and Learning and Skills Council (LSC) (2004), *Aim higher: guidance notes for integration.* HEFCE 2004/08, Bristol: HEFCE.

Higher Education Policy Institute (HEPI) (2003) *Widening participation and fair access: An overview of the evidence.* Oxford: HEPI.

Jackson, Brian and Marsden, D. (1966) *Education and the working class.* Harmondsworth: Penguin.

National Audit Office (NAO) (2002a) *Widening participation in higher education.* London: The Stationery Office.

National Audit Office (NAO) (2002b) *Improving student achievement in English higher education.* London: The Stationery Office.

Tomlinson Report (2003) *14–19: opportunity and excellence.* London: DfES.

Walker, I. and Zhu, Y. (2003) *Education, earnings and productivity: recent UK evidence*, in Labour Market Trends, Vol. III, No 3, March 2003.

Wolf, A. (2002) *Does Education Matter: Myths about Education and Economic Growth.* London: Penguin.

Chapter 1

Closing the equity gap: challenges of higher education

Geoff Layer

This book has arisen as a result of a wish to commemorate the life of Professor Colin Bell through the vehicle of one of his most loved pursuits – academic discovery and debate within the context of social inclusion. We have sought to produce a book which is based upon critical perspectives of the development of social inclusion within higher education in the UK and the USA based on a seminar which took place in Bradford, UK in March 2004.

Participation in education was a passionate interest of Colin's as he sought to create a more socially inclusive higher education in the universities in which he worked and across the sector as a whole. Colin participated in and led national and UK bodies that sought to influence change within our universities. He was an individual who believed in action and in making things happen through persuasion, culture change and, when necessary, that great change agent, *stealth*. Colleagues at Bradford always recounted stories that whenever you went to see Colin you came away feeling better but not really sure that you had achieved what you went in for in the first place. This was because he persuaded you of the need to take forward the institutional mission rather than that of the individual.

Colin was passionately supportive of widening participation and it was he who moved the University of Bradford's dated strap line away from 'Working towards equality of opportunity' to a new vision based on what he saw as the need for an inner-city university to engage very differently in a highly charged atmosphere. The new expression – 'Confronting Inequality: Celebrating Diversity' – is actually what Colin stood for. He was a champion of causes and wished to banish prejudice and discrimination. It was no surprise during his Vice-Chancellorship at Bradford that Rosemary Lawrence, the mother of Stephen Lawrence who was murdered in what many believe was a racially-motivated attack, received an honorary degree for her work in campaigning against institutional racism.

Colin's perspective on social inclusion was greater than that of a sociology researcher observing what happens and seeking to explain why such behaviour occurred. He really sought to make a difference and he did this through seeking to provide opportunities for people who were traditionally under-represented in society to achieve success. Colin always sought to achieve this through a process of 'main-streaming' the commitment and not through partial initiatives or 'bolt on' activities that the University could point at and say 'This is what we are doing.' He wanted to provide access to all subject areas and professions, hence Bradford's partnership with the University of Leeds, linking with local schools and focused on enabling under-represented groups to enter the medical profession, which has for years been one of the most conservative areas of higher education in terms of participation.

Colin though was always a pragmatist and a realist and knew that in many instances wholesale policy assaults were not always the most effective way to change conservative institutional practice. He was also well aware that change was often accepted at a policy level but obstructed in its implementation at the departmental or course level. This led to Colin always encouraging and welcoming experimental practice as a means of securing change. He therefore supported the notion of implementing ideas without necessarily going through a difficult bureaucratic approval process. Colin's encouragement when you told him about a particular success that had been delivered, but still required formal approval, was, so long as he liked the idea, to exclaim: 'It is always easier to ask for forgiveness for what you have done than to ask for permission to do it in the first place.'

By this he meant that, if a particular activity was meeting the university objectives, so long as it was within acceptable levels of practice you should do it and look for policy approval when you had the evidence to support it. This would prevent the conservative opposition delaying policy agreement so that the initiative could be put back until it had gone away, which can be a common trait within universities.

The subject of this book is one that explains approaches by higher education institutions and sector planners to the widening of participation in higher education (HE) in the UK and USA. The book is a collection of papers presented at a seminar held at the University of Bradford in March 2004 entitled 'Closing the Equity Gap: Is it sustainable?' The objectives of the seminar were to look at the factors critical to success or failure in closing the 'equity gap in HE' and looking at the commonality of themes for policymakers and practitioners. This book reflects those seminar papers and includes the Colin Bell Memorial Lecture by Sir Howard Newby, an overview of participation by Professor Sir David Watson, and six other papers from UK/USA researchers and a concluding chapter identifying the main conclusions from the discussion.

The concept of widening participation is a much contested one among academics across higher education nationally and internationally. Some schools of thought argue that universities should base their recruitment simply on identifiable academic excellence. Others argue that there is a need for universities to be more socially inclusive and to reflect the different starting points of under-represented groups. These are two extremes of the argument and many seek to reconcile the two perspectives into the middle ground. There is, however, no reason why the widening of participation should have any impact on the strategy to recruit being based on academic excellence. The challenge identified in this book is for the sector to seek to ensure that academic excellence does not become confused with the ability to pay, or to simply rely on a model of recruitment and progression based on a narrow perception of academic preparation and excellence. Similarly a theme which is taken up by most contributors is that higher education does not stand still and needs to address the changing nature of the student community. The argument put forward is that the curriculum needs to reflect the needs of the learner and to address their starting point, not the starting point that the institution or lecturer may assume. This may mean different forms of higher education provision and alternative routes into and through universities. This perceived divide between the two camps, which is a constant part of the debate, is a distraction as the key issue is to focus on the purpose and the values of higher education:

> A modern higher education sector must be open and inclusive. It must pursue wider social inclusion as an institutional objective.
>
> Blunkett (2000)

This is much easier to pronounce on than it is to deliver. It is all very well to lead the political call for greater inclusivity on a system-wide basis, but there is a pressing need to ensure that the purpose and the means are clearly identified as well. It is equally important that not only do universities look to be more socially inclusive in respect of participation levels but that they secure the internal change necessary to make sure that the target groups are supported to enable the achievement of success. This is often referred to as the 'access to what' debate or as Stuart (2000) says:

> My worry is not about widening our massification, but rather about the terms of participation: in other words, what is there to participate in and how is the power balance of participation addressed?

This 'access to what' debate is part of the reason why Action on Access, a national organisation that was established to support widening participation in HE, which Bell chaired, has always argued that widening participation can never simply focus on entry routes and process but must look at helping the student to succeed. This was recognised when the Higher Education Funding Council for England (HEFCE) called upon universities and colleges in England to provide more holistic widening participation strategies (HEFCE, 2001: Action on Access, 2002). The HEFCE strategic plan in 2003 included a chapter on widening participation and reflected on the student life cycle model developed by Action on Access (Figure 1.1).

Figure 1.1: Student life cycle

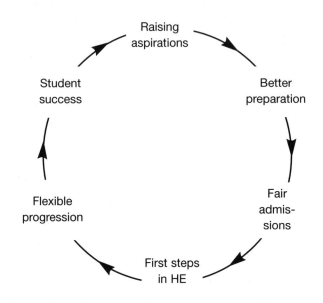

(Source: HEFCE Strategic Plan, July 2003.)

The essays in this book reflect much of Bell's perspective on the need for informed debate, the need to look at the evidence of what was happening and the impact this had on behaviour.

In the Colin Bell Memorial Lecture, Newby provides an analysis of how institutions operate and the challenges they face in seeking a more inclusive higher education sector. In this chapter Newby reflects on his life working with Bell and then moves on to consider some of the implications of the current UK system in which, although 90 per cent of young people with A-levels enter HE, there is a significant social class distinction between those who actually present themselves for admission to degrees and those who do not. Newby clearly rules out any lowering of standards as a means of reaching the communities that are not currently participating but is clear that more needs to be achieved on both the demand and the supply side of the equation. In terms of demand he acknowledges the need to focus on the raising of attainment levels in schools where young people from lower socio-economic groups are disproportionately clustered and for universities and colleges to work with schools and colleges on an outreach basis to help to raise aspirations.

On the supply side though, Newby is more demanding, calling for an end to the confused progression routes scenario in UK higher education and emphasising the need for a new agenda in which progression routes exist on a planned basis, with transfer arrangements available to support learning, not just institutional priorities. This reflects a shift for the sector in moving from a provider-led model to one which has greater emphasis on building and responding to demand. This call for planning is based on many of the valuable lessons from appropriate parts of the North American model.

In Chapter 2 Watson presents an overview of trends and challenges in participation within higher education. He introduces an interesting comparison of participation data across the European Union, reflects on other comparators across the world and asks some particularly challenging questions. He starts by unpicking the Trow (1989) model of the distinctions between 'elite, mass and universal' systems of higher education and demonstrates that the rapid shift from elite to universal did not really pause to take account of a mass system.

Watson makes a very strong case that in order to widen participation in higher education it needs to be able to expand in order to create wider opportunity and to provide the appropriate infrastructure. Watson's analysis shows that in the UK, when compared to the European Union, we have greater numbers of older, part-time and disabled students. None of this success actually required higher levels of lower socio-economic group participation and that is why expansion is necessary to achieve further success within that group. Watson presents the reader with seven hard questions about the system and identifies five traps to avoid.

In Chapter 4 Parry explores the history and the progress made in establishing an HE culture within FE colleges, particularly in England. Parry's account of the scale of change over the last 20 years in terms of structural change with the role of colleges in HE tending to always fall off the agenda raises the question of how it has managed to survive. It is important to recognise the contribution made by the college sector when it is typically faced with lower units of resource and an absence of a policy agenda. One of the stark factors in Parry's analysis is the lack of planning within the FE sector, as there is a combination of a concentration of provision in some colleges and a widespread distribution of low numbers of students. It is also evident that there is an absence of planning of links between universities and colleges and this identifies the need for Newby's call for the establishment of Lifelong Learning Networks.

In his paper looking at the Changing Politics of College Access in the United States (Chapter 3), Mumper traces the impact of the political changes that have affected the engagement of lower income groups in higher education. At a time when colleges' prices are rising Mumper finds that the gap between the participation rates of those from lower income groups and those from upper income groups is increasing despite greater government spending on support. Mumper explains the shift in college access policy since 1965 through the 1980s and 90s in demonstrating the shift from the affirmative and targeted approach to the broader universalist framework. The affirmative admission policies of the 1960s have been gradually eroded and are now generally replaced by a 'race-blind' admission approach and there has subsequently been a significant drop in minority ethnic participation in the most selective institutions.

Alongside this shift away from positive and affirmative approaches to admission has come a shift away from financial support targeted on low income groups to a more universal approach of subsidy to all. The impact of this shift towards supporting middle and upper income groups has fuelled an increase in college prices and seen the lower income groups focus more on two-year courses at public bodies rather than courses at some of the more selective institutions. Individual state systems have also introduced 'merit' awards which again favour the better-off. Mumper makes a very strong case for the inequity of the universal approach in a system that was designed for targeted support. This shift appears as part of the social welfare policy change in the USA towards benefits for more of the population. In higher education the change simply leads to less meaningful access for the poorer members of society.

Field, in Chapter 5, examines the blurring of boundaries across different aspects of the post-compulsory sectors and the expansion of short cycle higher education outside of universities. He draws on comparisons between a range of European countries and North America in looking at HE provision in the college sectors. The main thrust of the paper is an assessment of the progress made with short cycle HE in Scotland. This is the country in the UK which has already achieved 50 per cent participation but, as Field establishes, there are significant differences in who is participating and in what is being accessed across Scotland. The growth in HE participation in Scotland has been in Higher National courses in the colleges rather than in the universities. Typically the take-up of this short cycle vocational provision is from the lower socio-economic groups, is part-time and leads to a particular type of job. Increasingly as a result of the development of ScotCAT, the credit accumulation and transfer scheme adopted in Scotland, more comprehensive articulation arrangements between colleges and universities leading to progression to degree courses are beginning to take effect. However, as Field points out, these are differential in scale and scope. This, coupled with the very different levels of completion between the Higher Nationals and degree courses, does mean that there are still significant questions to be answered. Again there is a theme throughout this analysis of 'What is the access to?' and the extent to which it is comparable or whether it needs to be considered in a different way.

In Chapter 6 Baum assesses the economic perspective of widening participation based on experience within the USA. Baum uses the tools of economic analysis to look at how the interventions that are made can have an impact on inequality. The analysis particularly looks at the impact of price sensitivity and price differentiation and any significance they have in terms of achieving participation. It raises the very difficult political and social issue of whether financial support for the take-up of higher education by students is based on individual financial need for poorer students or whether it has become a more general financial support system for all. Thus the argument here is whether a price-driven commodity in the state system actually exists or whether the State is actually subsidising the cost for all to participate. Baum also focuses on the key economic argument of 'choice' and whether the 'choice' that is taking place is about 'where and how to participate' or fundamentally 'whether to participate'. Interestingly though, Baum does not just consider the significance of simply participation to HE and takes a more holistic approach. This is an example of the shift that the book promotes to looking at 'access to what' by looking at completion rates and the distinction between the impact on those from the lowest family income quartile and those from the highest.

Stuart in Chapter 7 moves the debate on and away from a focus on participation to one of addressing learning and teaching within higher education. Stuart reflects on the work undertaken by Action on Access which has sought to persuade the UK HE sector that, in order to widen participation fully, not only do you need to address the issue of who is participating and ensuring greater inclusion but you need to address the issue of the curriculum. The challenge here for universities is whether the curriculum they have developed, which was originally designed around an elite system with a specific level of knowledge required in a discipline, is appropriate for a mass or universal system where the starting point of the learner may be so different from that of the elite model. That is not to say one system is better than another but to recognise diversity within the sector and among the learners. Stuart is effectively arguing that the curriculum should be designed to reflect where the student is starting from rather than where the provider wants them to be.

Stuart reflects on a comparison with the Rust belt, which is an example of the impact of a post-industrial society in which the industrial base has declined and been replaced with a service industry culture which has major impact on the gender of the workforce, the skill level required and its casualisation. When translated into an educational setting it leads to higher education needing to transform itself and to be more engaged with its learning communities. This then means that the academics and the supporting system need to take account of broad social issues and prior learning, all of which is a major cultural transformation.

In Chapter 8 McCormick looks at the successes and challenges of the Access agenda in the USA and addresses the mismatch between recruitment and completion most succinctly. This analysis also focuses on the participation and retention of students from low socio-economic groups. In his section on 'who participates and where' McCormick explores some of the crucial issues about who is actually participating. He clearly finds that more students from the lower socio-economic groups have the ability and the capacity to benefit from higher education than are currently doing so. This he argues is not about preparation for higher education but more about expectation and culture. In focusing on what happens to students once they enter higher education, McCormick looks at 'enrolment persistence and degree completion'. As retention is highest in the most selective institutions, which the middle- and higher-income students tend to favour, he argues that the benefits they receive are higher than those for the lower income groups attending the least selective institutions.

The book concludes with a chapter reporting on the debates and conclusions from the seminar and the discussion. It is evident from this work that in both the UK and the USA we are at one of those important moments that will determine participation over the next decade. In both cases it is quite clear from the evidence argued here that the new frameworks require a focus on targeted financial support, developed progression routes, change within the curriculum and expansion of the system. Without these we may still hit Trow's universal levels of participation but it will be a disjointed and socially uncomfortable experience.

References

Blunkett, D. (2000) *Higher Education in the Twenty-first Century.* 15th February, University of Greenwich.

Higher Education Funding Council for England (2001) *Strategies for Widening Participation in HE, A guide to good practice*, Circular 01/36 (Bristol: HEFCE).

Higher Education Funding Council for England (2003) *Strategic Plan 2003–08*, Circular 03/12 (Bristol: HEFCE).

Layer, G., Stuart, M. and Srivastava, A. (2003) *Student Success Strategy*, Action on Access.

Stuart, M. (2000) Beyond Rhetoric: reclaiming a radical agenda for active participation in Higher Education. In: *Stretching the Academy*, J. Thompson, Leicester, NIACE.

Trow, M. (1989) 'The Robbins Trap: British Attitudes and the Limits of Expansion', *Higher Education Quarterly*, Vol. 43, No 1, pp. 55–75.

Chapter 2

Overview: telling the truth about widening participation

David Watson

Introduction

These papers, and the discussion to which they led, represent an attempt at tackling perhaps the hardest question facing the university system around the world at the beginning of its eighth century. That question is about how we achieve equity at the same time as excellence in our institutions, in our national systems, and in the global community of higher education. I try in this chapter to draw together some of the threads. However, I would like to begin with a brief personal note.

We are all going to have to find our own ways to pay tribute to the memory of our friend and colleague Colin Bell. The quality Colin had of which I have been most conscious in preparing this presentation was his courage. He was quite literally fearless in following difficult ideas towards their conclusion, and not only expressing but living with the consequences. He thus helped the system, and those of us within it who might be tempted to trim, not only to tell truth to power (not nearly as hard in the comfortable West as it is for many of our counterparts in universities elsewhere in the world), but to tell truth to ourselves. The latter is especially hard in professionally argumentative communities like universities, where arrogance can so easily be mistaken for integrity. He was a scholar and a leader; and he demonstrated that it was possible to be both.

Widening participation: the big picture

The one absolutely iron law about widening participation is that if you want the system to be fairer it has to be allowed to expand.

Table 2.1 (named after Martin Trow) shows how we used to look at expansion. It was devised in the context of a theory (the Robbins Trap) that was actually about 'pulling up the ladder'. Trow's advice to the UK was that if you let more people in you must reduce your ambition about the kind of experience they will have.

Table 2.1: Trow's taxonomy

- elite systems enrol up to 15% of the age group
- mass systems enrol 15–40% of the age group
- universal systems enrol more than 40% of the age group

(Source: Brennan, 2004.)

There are two problems here. The first is parochial: the Robbins Trap never in fact materialised in the UK, largely because of the performance of polytechnics, colleges, and subsequently the 'new new' universities. They have subsequently largely maintained their missions in respect of professional and vocational courses, and service to local and regional communities, along with development of applied research, sometimes of real distinction (as in art and design) (see Watson and Bowden, 2002). The second is universal and is contained in the data from the OECD in Figure 2.1. It is apparent that so-called elite university education exists hardly anywhere in the world, and that most major systems are closing in on the 'universal' target. The global and historical truth about 'mass' higher education is that if you blinked you would have missed it.

Also bear in mind that this figure is about 'completion' of first level higher education, and not just – as in Trow's analysis – enrolments. As Thomas Weko demonstrates, until very recently little attention was paid in the USA to 'completion' or its reciprocal, 'wastage' (legislators have been catching up fast). Weko's theory is that this is cultural: 'in the US view, completing a degree is better than not, but something is better than nothing' (Weko, 2004).

Figure 2.1 Ratio of tertiary graduates to the population at the typical age of graduation (2001): for all type A programmes (first time graduation)

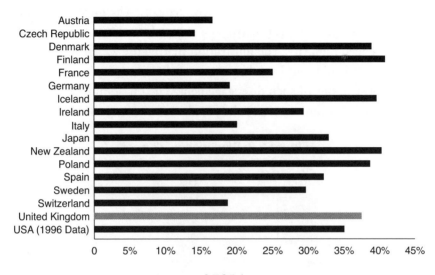

(Source: Education at a glance – OECD.)

Hard questions

So if Trow and his Robbins trap are history, what are the hard questions about widening participation all around the world? I think that they reduce to seven.

1. *The question of polarisation*

   The more successful that national systems are in growing participation and achievement, the greater will be the gap between those who stay on a ladder of educational attainment and those who drop off. We have solid, longitudinal data about the positive effects of participation on not only work, but health, happiness and democratic tolerance. I would refer you particularly to the output of the Wider Benefits of Learning (WBL) group at the Institute of Education (Bynner et al., 2003; Schuller et al., 2004). We have a lot of international hand-wringing about 'completion' (or its opposite, 'wastage'). And it is true that the WBL group does invalidate part of the Weko thesis, by showing the negative effect – particularly on young working-class males – of enrolling in but then dropping out of higher education. But the big picture is that we don't talk enough about 're-starting' or 're-engagement.' The most important issue is the growing gulf between a successful majority and a disengaged minority. The illustration that Figure 2.2 provides is now a little old, but I think it is one of the most graphic demonstrations of such disengagement. The question that follows is 'Is higher education part of the problem, or part of the solution?'

Figure 2.2: Work rich/work poor

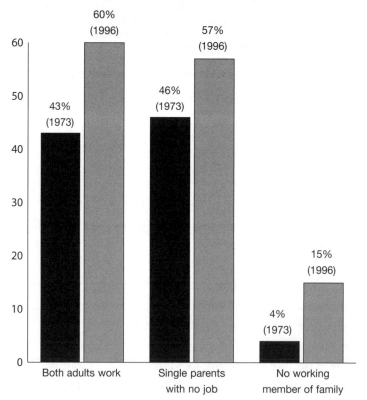

(Source: Berthoud and Gershuny, 2000.)

2. *Growing the qualified cohort*
   Meanwhile, higher education (HE) advocates are very good at displacement of responsibility – and one of their most plausible

fields for this is about retention and achievement in school. 'We can't admit them unless they prepare them.' They are less ready to assume their part of the responsibility for the schools themselves, and disabling features of the communities they are trying to support.

There are cross-national comparative issues which are also crucial here, such as the effective school-leaving age (the UK is one of the last major developed countries to have an effective school-leaving age at 16), and mathematics in the later years of compulsory schooling (equally, we are probably unique in not requiring a mathematical qualification as part of general university matriculation).

3. *The question of class*
   It is not quite universally true (because of local cultural circumstances), but the weight of the evidence suggests that the key divide around the world is no longer gender, or ethnicity (except in special circumstances); it is also decreasingly about disability. The key determinant is good, old-fashioned socio-economic circumstances; in short it is class. In the USA, the President of Harvard has taken the lead in refocusing equal opportunities on economic disadvantage (see Julianne Basinger and Scott Smallwood in the *Chronicle of Higher Education* [*CHE*], 1.3.04). Meanwhile, the American research agenda has shifted from William Bowen and Derek Bok's seminal work on race, *The Shape of the River* (1998), to Richard Kallenberg's work on low-income students, *The Untapped Resource* (2004).

   In the UK we know that 90 per cent of students with two or more A-levels go on to higher education. Table 2.2 presents some data about class and 'high-fliers' (those with exceptional A-level results). It shows how heavily the top results are concentrated among the most affluent families.

4. *Who are the minorities?*
   There is a particular resonance to my third question as New Labour seeks to put the concept of 'under-represented groups' on

Table 2.2: 2001 year of entry. Total number of all applicants by social class and grade

Grade	30 to 26 pts
Social class	ALL APPLICANTS
I Professional	13,117
II Intermediate	25,177
IIIM Skilled manual	5,468
IIIN Skilled non-manual	5,493
IV Partly skilled	2,135
V Unskilled	459
X Unknown	2,556
Total	54,405

Notes: .1 Country: UK (Source: UCAS.)

the face of its 2004 Higher Education Act. Turn the question on its head, and look at local cultural and political hang-ups. Who, in fact, is meant to be left outside?

Let me refer you to several controversies in contemporary international higher education which are in fact about purportedly protecting majorities against minorities (see Beth McMurtie in *CHE*, 13.2.04). In China, in contrast to the admission advantage given to speakers of 55 minority languages, there is official discrimination against students with physical disabilities (see Jiang Zuequin in *CHE*, 26.7.04). British universities know that in large part their success in recruiting from Pacific Rim countries arises from the legal preference given to indigenous groups which causes a disproportionate number of the Chinese minority to seek their HE overseas. In Israel there has been a political U-turn over entrance tests, as their abandonment has apparently not advantaged working-class Jews but Arab-Israelis instead (see Chris McGreal in *The Guardian* 1.12.03; and Haim Watzman in the *CHE*, 26.3.04). In Hungary, on the eve of accession to the EU, only 0.22 per cent of the country's gypsies get as far as college (see Colin Woodard in the *CHE*, 19.3.04). In Japan, Wako University has revoked its offer of admission to the daughter of the leader of the Aum Shinriko sect (the perpetrator of the 1995 Sarin gas attack). She and her siblings have renounced the sect, but, in the words of the President 'she is likely to prompt uneasiness' and 'there may also be criticism from society' (see Alan Brender in the *CHE*, 22.4.04). See also Chris McGreal in *The Guardian* 1.12.03 and stories in the *CHE*, 19/22/26.03.04. At any point in time there may be consensus about who the 'under-represented' groups are, but it is surely a dangerous hostage to political fashion; 'degrees for votes' could perhaps follow in the footsteps of 'homes for votes'.

5. *Access to what?*

There is also the critical issue of what the 'new' students in higher education do, and what its value turns out to be for their careers and their quality of life. A recent report from the Open University's Centre for Higher Education Research & Information (CHERI) with this title concluded that in the UK 'background disadvantages still seem to give rise to employment disadvantages, even when the effects of institution, subject, entry qualifications and degree class have been taken into account' (Brennan and Shah, 2003: iii). As we have made HE fairer, we have only further exposed patterns of discrimination in employment (as the UK Council for Industry and Higher Education [CIHE], to their credit, have consistently pointed out [CIHE, 2002]).

Interestingly, 'access to what?' is also a question posed by the American National Center for Postsecondary Improvement in its recent policy paper, *Beyond Dead Reckoning*, who also expose some of the key pedagogical issues (NCPI, 2002).

6. *Equality vs excellence*

In February 2001, the House of Commons Education and Employment Committee concluded their report on Higher Education: Access, with the following statement: 'Our values and our democratic commitments press us to answer the old question "Can we be equal and excellent too?" with a resounding "yes"' (para. 116).

To return to my opening theme: the hard fact is that it's easier to invest in excellence (however you define it, and in the UK we have a thing called the Research Assessment Exercise [RAE]), than in equality. The expanding differential between funding research and funding teaching (including infrastructure) in England seems inexorable: between 2002–03 and 2003–04 the funding for research has grown by over 10 per cent. That for teaching has grown by less than 3 per cent, while the projections for the period covered by the government White Paper, *The Future of Higher Education*, show a fall in real terms funding per student of 0.6 per cent between 2002–03 and 2005–06 (unpublished analysis by UUK, 2003).

7. *The admissions header tank*

Another candidate for a universal truth is that institutions almost everywhere will admit the students which it is easiest and most profitable to recruit and then go looking for the rest. This is true within as well as between universities, to an extent that it will hardly be touched by the mild meliorism of the UK's Schwartz Commission (DfES, 2004). Another hazard is the UK's rose-tinted view of 'needs-blind' selection by American elite universities, as recent muck-raking volumes attest. These include James Steinberg's *The Gatekeepers: inside the admissions process of a premier college*, on Wesleyan, and Christopher Avery, Andrew Fairbanks and Richard Zeckhauser's *The Early Admissions Game on Harvard* (see also the article by Louis Menand in *The New Yorker*, 7.4.03, 'The Thin Envelope').

'Nobody's perfect'

No system has all of the answers. A large section of the seminar reported in this volume is about comparative performance, and chiefly on an Anglo-American axis. I would like to take the opportunity to introduce a dimension we rarely tackle, which is a comparison of participation indices across the European Union. The data (analysed by Brian Ramsden) is based upon a study called 'EuroStudent 2000', which the UK government declined the opportunity to join (Slowey and Watson, 2003, pp. 3–19).

It's interesting to note that, compared to the rest of the (current) EU, we have: the highest percentage of part-time students (see Figure 2.3);the highest average age of participants (Figure 2.4); the highest percentage with disabilities (Figure 2.5) (although classification is notoriously difficult here); and the second highest rate of working-class participation (Figure 2.6) (behind Finland, one of the most 'planned systems' in the EU).

We also have: the lowest rate of 'study from home, after Finland (Figure 2.7) and the second lowest 'regional' effect of recruitment (Figure 2.8).

It is interesting to reflect on how this pattern may be changed by the 'accession' states (and some useful preliminary work has been done by the Higher Education Policy Institute [HEPI, 2004]). I anticipate not much. In the meantime, it's worth reflecting on why (despite all of our legitimate concerns about equity), the UK seems to do comparatively well. As Figure 2.9 indicates, this may have something to do with the diversity of our provision (the thing that Martin Trow says that we

Figure 2.3: 'Part-time' students as a percentage of all *(Ibid: p. 7.)*

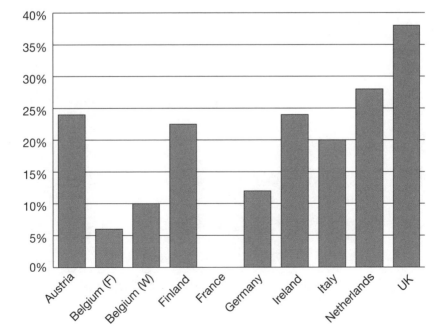

Figure 2.4: Average age of undergraduate students *(Ibid: p. 9.)*

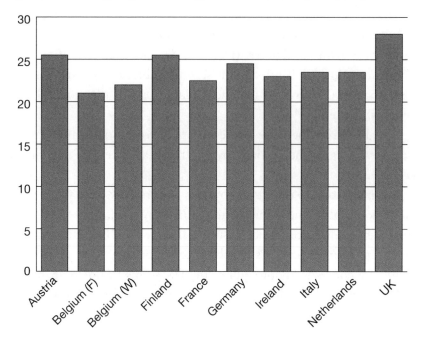

Figure 2.5: Percentage of students with disabilities *(Ibid: p. 11.)*

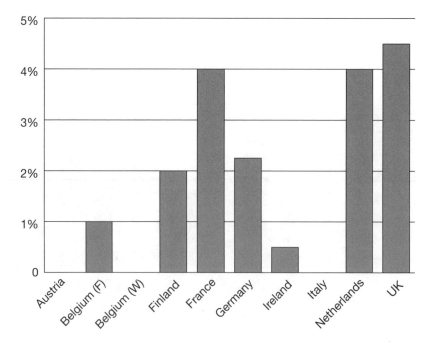

Figure 2.6: Percentage of students from lower socio-economic groups *(Ibid: p. 15.)*

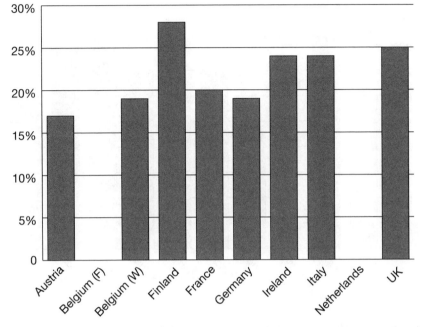

Figure 2.7: Percentage of students occupying institutional and parental accommodation *(Ibid: p. 16.)*

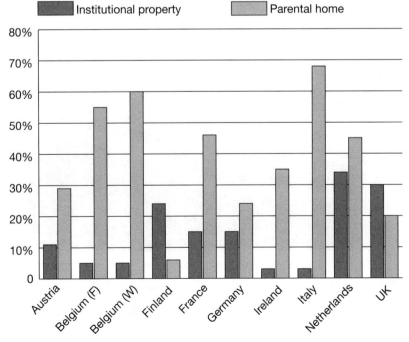

Figure 2.8: Estimated regionalisation rate *(Ibid: p. 17.)*

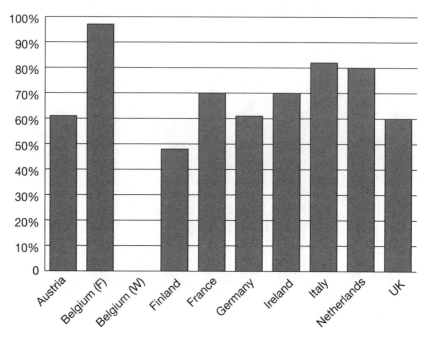

Figure 2.9: Student numbers by level and mode
(Source: Slowey and Watson, 2003: xxiv.)

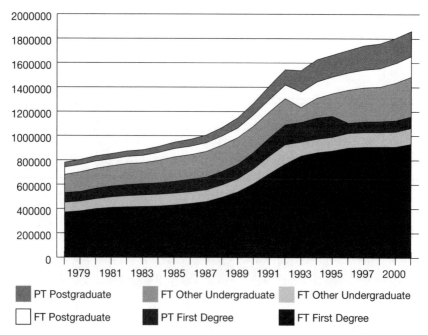

lack). Looking from the United States to the UK, the latter may seem less diverse and more fixed into a traditional mould. Looking from the UK to Europe puts everything in an entirely different light.

Inclusion is hard

So, to sum up: inclusion *is* hard, and as with all varieties of affirmative action it raises 'wicked' issues. Here is another list of traps I think we must avoid.

1. *Cherry-picking*

   Higher education systems are (as John Kay says of markets) 'culturally embedded'. You can't select some features of other people's frameworks which you like, and ignore the others. Tony Blair, as British Prime Minister, is one of the latest to fail to walk around this particular elephant trap. As he said in January 2004: 'There are certain features of the US system which we emphatically do not want to emulate, in particular escalating fees to attend certain universities, and the absence of a proper nationwide grant and deferred fee scheme' (Tony Blair to Institute for Public Policy Research, 14.1.04).

   There are two other Trow traps here. First that you can do it on the cheap, as with the enthusiasm – shared by many within the UK – for short cycle HE in FE institutions. The Scottish data should give us real pause here: HE in FE in Scotland (as proud as Scotland is of its superior participation rate) has led to under-funding, incompletion dand demonstrable lack of fairness in progression. Secondly, the California state system hardly remains a model. Here we have the header tank theory applying in spades: as the state budget has been squeezed, the equity commitments in the Master Plan have fallen by the wayside. David Kirp has recently reported that for spring 2004 entry, the University of California returned 2,000 transfer applications unread, while the California state system rejected 30,000 qualified applicants for transfer (*Crosstalk* 12:1, 11–12).

   Other people's higher education systems in fact come in

45

Table 2.3: Higher education features

Features	Europe	N. America	'Expanded UK'
	MODELS		
Institutional characteristics	large	variable size	relatively small
	uniform	highly stratified	guaranteed standards
Student experience	free tuition	variable costs	state support
	study from home	work-study	away from home
	rationed facilities	variable facilities	controlled range of facilities
Curriculum	long courses	varied pace of study	intensive courses
	qualification filters	general u.g. 'professional' p.g.	general and professional' u.g.
Outcomes	low completion	delayed completion	high completion

(Source: Watson, 1998.)

inconvenient packages, as I set out in Table 2.3, based upon an analysis before the Dearing Inquiry.

2. *Fuzzy thinking*

The big trap in the UK at the moment is the illusion that 'aiming higher' and 'widening participation' are the same thing. Table 2.4 presents another take on the A-level data I offered earlier. Note that the bottom group has fewer successes, lower achievement, but the same progression rate with that achievement. (There's also a gender effect, with girls pulling away from boys at every level of UK public examinations after the first SATs.)

Table 2.4: UK education experience by socio-economic group

	Less affluent background (III-manual IV and V)		More affluent background (I, II, and III non-manual)	
Percentage gaining 2+ A/AS levels	23%	47%		
subdivided into:				
25+ points	6%	(26%)	18%	(38%)
13–24 points	11%	(48%)	21%	(45%)
1–12 points	6%	(26%)	8%	(17%)
Percentage entering HE:				
25+ points	71%	73%		
13–24 points	57%	62%		
1–12 points	45%	45%		

Notes:
1 Youth Cohort Study (Cohort 10, Sweep 3, 18-year-olds in 2002)
2 Percentages of 18-year-olds in each group
(HE covers all full- and part-time study at degree and other level 4 qualifications and above.)
(Source: DfES, Youth Cohort Study, 2002.)

3. *The squeaky wheel*

This trap relates particularly to funding decisions. It's easier to fund institutions on the 'reward' than the 'compensation' principle – and this is how research beats widening participation every time. And it's easier to comfort the middle class than genuinely to target student support where it is needed. As Jamil Salmi, co-ordinator of the World Bank's Tertiary Education Group, said in 2000: 'I tell the governments I work with that you can't look at tuition independently from student aid. I think any country can create a student aid program if they are serious about it. The technical challenges aren't that great. The problem is that many societies don't have the political will to discriminate against the children of the rich' (*CHE*, 5.5.00).

4. *Blaming other people*

Universities can (with justice) point accusations in two directions: towards compulsory schooling for not providing the entrants and towards employers for failing to respond to a more diverse and democratic body of graduates. In the twenty-first century, however, we have to ask what we can do to help to put both problems right.

5. *Short-termism*

Above all, we have to be realistic about the long haul. I think that much of this reduces to political consensus and political courage (and I'm aware that I can be accused of another form of displacement). Higher education participation, at the levels now being achieved around the world, does relate to healthier, happier, more tolerant societies (a point completely missed, for example, by Alison Wolf in her attack on HE expansion in Does Education Matter? [2002]). In the UK in particular, this argument has not yet been won. It will be, but only as we reach a level of graduates in society who can insist upon it.

References

Berthoud, R. and Gershuny, J. (eds) (2000) *Seven Years in the Lives of British Families; evidence on the dynamics of social change from the British Household Panel Survey*. Bristol: The Policy Press

Brennan, J. (2004) The Social Role of the Contemporary University; contradictions, boundaries and change. In *Ten Years On: changing higher education in a changing world*. London: CHERI (Centre for Higher Education Research and Information): pp. 22–6.

Brennan, J. and Shah, T. (2003) *Access to What? Converting educational opportunity into employment opportunity*. London: CHERI.

Bynner, J., Dolton, P., Feinstein L., Makepiece, G., Malmberg, L. and Woods, L. (2003) *Revisiting the Benefits of Higher Education: a report by the Bedford Group for Lifecourse and Statistical Studies, Institute of Education*. Bristol: HEFCE.

Council for Industry and Higher Education (CIHE) (2002) *Recruiting from a Wider Spectrum of Graduates*. London: CIHE.

Department for Education and Skills (DfES) (2004) *Fair admissions to higher education: draft recommendations for consultation*. DfES/Admissions to Higher Education Steering Group, April.

Higher Education Policy Institute (HEPI) *Projecting Demand for UK Higher Education from the Accession Countries*. HEPI Report Summary 8: Oxford, March.

Kay, J. (2003) *The Truth about Markets: their genius, their limits, their follies*. London: Allen Lane.

Learning & Skills Research Centre (LSRC) (2002) *Saving for Learning Strand 2: an international comparison*. Taunton: LSRC.

National Center for Postsecondary Improvement (NCPI) (2002) *Beyond Dead Reckoning; research priorities for redirecting American Higher Education*. Stanford, Ca. NCPI:

OECD (2003) *Education at a Glance*. Paris: OECD.

Schuller, T., Preston, J., Hammond, C., Brassett-Grundy, A. and Bynner, J. (2004) *The Benefits of Learning: the impact of education on health, family life and social capital*. London: Routledge Falmer.

Slowey, M. and Watson, D. (2003) *Higher Education and the Lifecourse*. Maidenhead: SRHE and Open University Press.

Trow, M. (1989) 'The Robbins Trap: British attitudes and the limits of expansion', *Higher Education Quarterly*, Vol.. 41, No 3, pp. 268–92.

Watson, D. (1998) The Limits to Diversity. In D. Jary and M. Parker, *The New Higher Education: issues and directions for the post-Dearing university*. Stafford: Staffordshire University Press.

Watson, D. and Bowden, R. (2002) *The New University Decade, 1992–2002*. University of Brighton Education Research Centre Occasional Paper (September).

Weko, T. (2004) *New Dogs and Old Tricks: what can the UK teach the US about university education?* Mimeo: March.

Wolf, A. (2002) *Does Education Matter? Myths about education and economic growth.* London: Penguin.

Chapter 3

The changing politics of college access in the United States

Michael Mumper

Access to higher education for disadvantaged families in the United States has been declining since the early 1980s. While public college prices are up substantially, family incomes are flat and the purchasing power of need-based financial aid is down. The college participation gap between lower- and upper-income families is higher than it has been since before the enactment of the Higher Education Act in 1965. Yet, these trends are not the result of a massive reduction in government spending for higher education. State appropriations to higher education are up each year. While state support has not kept pace with the increase in spending of public universities, it has grown at a steady pace. At the same time, federal spending on higher education has increased substantially. In particular, the enactment of the HOPE and Lifelong Learning tax credits represent dramatic increases in federal support for higher education. These two divergent patterns, more government spending to produce less college access, are a matter of national concern. As Congress prepares to reauthorise the Higher Education Act, several members have been sharply critical of the lack of progress towards the goal of improving college access.

Why has the USA experienced such dramatic differences in the relative college access of students from different economic backgrounds in spite of substantial spending on college access programmes? I argue that beginning in the mid-1960s, federal, state, and institutional efforts to improve college access coalesced into what I term the Great Society Design. This combination of low public college tuition, generous federal need-based student aid, and affirmative action admissions policies produced improvements in the college participation of low-income students that lasted throughout the 1970s. But beginning around 1980, this design began to unravel. The goal of improving college access for disadvantaged students was never explicitly renounced or replaced. But after more than 20 years of tinkering with state, federal, and institutional policies the Great Society Design has been transformed into something altogether different. Today, the primary policy goal of improving college access for low-income students has been quietly replaced by the goal of improving college affordability for middle- and upper-income students. This goal displacement has been accompanied by a fundamental shift in the allocation of government subsidies. Over time, a smaller and smaller portion of those subsidies is targeted to the most needy students and new programmes have been put in place that target benefits directly to middle-income students. It is not the case that government policy has failed to achieve the goal of improved access. Government policies implicitly abandoned that goal many years ago, and replaced it with the different goal of improved affordability.

In this paper, I explore the transformation of college access policy since 1965. I begin by reviewing the development of the original Great Society Design in the 1960s. I then examine how, beginning in 1980, that design was quietly transformed into the present system.

Some of the reasons for these changes were straightforward. The designers of the Great Society programmes were replaced by a new generation of elected officials who did not share the same vision or values. Moreover, even those who may have supported the goal of access were persuaded that government support should be spread more broadly among all income groups. The voices of middle- and upper-income students are more clearly heard in legislatures than those of the disadvantaged. But another change was also at work. A new philosophy emerged about how best to design effective social policies. The view that support should be targeted to the most needy was replaced by the 'universalist' view that policies should be designed to provide support to the widest possible spectrum of society. These new policy makers, political pressures, and the new approach to policy design, combined to facilitate the replacement of the Great Society Design with a system of spiralling tuition, middle-class tax credits, and merit scholarship entitlements. Finally, I review some of the important consequences that transformation has had on college access for the disadvantaged. Research shows that a combination of misdirected government subsidies in the existing programmes, the creation of inappropriately designed new programmes, and the changing demographics of college students are on the verge of undermining the role of public higher education in advancing equal opportunity.

The Great Society Design

Beginning in the 1960s, state governments, the Federal Government, and public colleges and universities developed a loosely coordinated partnership to increase college participation among the disadvantaged in which each level assumed a complementary role. State governments provided public campuses with sufficient funds to ensure that tuition costs remained low. The Federal Government developed an extensive system of need-based grants to college students to ensure that all students who could be admitted to college could afford at attend. And individual institutions implemented admissions policies that gave advantages to students from racial minorities or with disadvantaged backgrounds. While it was never explicitly planned, this combination of low tuition, grant assistance, and preferential admissions policies helped to increase access to college for the target populations throughout the late 1960s and 1970s (Heller, 1999).

The role of state government

The traditional state role in maintaining equal educational opportunity was to maintain low public college tuition. This was done by providing generous subsidies for campuses which, in turn, used those funds to keep prices low. In a 1971 analysis of the relationship between prices and college admissions, Christopher Jenks found that the situation of the disadvantaged student improved between 1900 and the 1950s.

> During the first half of the twentieth century the combined cost of room, board, and tuition rose considerably more slowly than family incomes. This meant that a substantially larger proportion of the population could afford to attend college in 1950 than at any previous time.
>
> (Jenks, 1971, p. 88)

These long periods of low tuition at public colleges in many states did not happen by accident. It was the result of a sustained effort by state policy makers to provide public higher education at the lowest feasible cost. Indeed, a number of states have constitutional provisions that mandate such practices. This low tuition approach was possible because the cost of providing higher education was relatively low, at least by today's standards. In addition, the portion of the population attending public colleges was relatively small.

These conditions changed in the second half of the century and public college tuition began to increase in the 1970s. Those price increases accelerated in the early 1980s. Figures 3.1 and 3.2 show the average tuition and fees charged at two- and four-year public colleges and universities. Between the 1981–82 and 2001–02 academic years, constant dollar tuition increased by 183 per cent at a public four-year college. Figure 3.2 shows that during that same period, the increase was 112 per cent at a public two-year college. The reasons for these increases have been the source of much controversy. In 1998, Congress was so concerned that it established the National Commission on the Costs of Higher Education to conduct a comprehensive review of college costs and prices. After months of hearings and staff investigation, the Commission concluded but reached no consensus (National Commission on the Costs of Higher Education, 1999). Some observers place the blame for rising tuition on declining levels of state support for higher education. While total state support to public colleges has increased steadily since 1980, the rate of increase has been slower than that of personal income or state spending in general. The result has been that state appropriations have declined as a portion of

Figure 3.1: Average tuition and fees at four-year public colleges, enrolment weighted (US $)

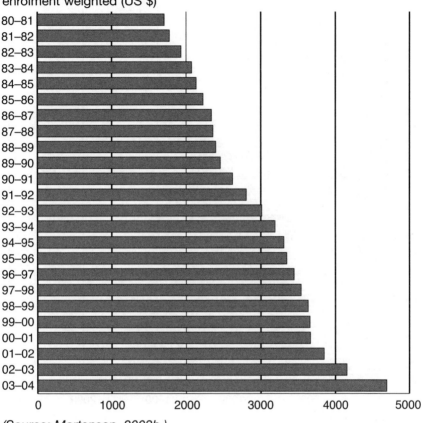

(Source: Mortenson, 2003b.)

the revenue received by public colleges. Campus leaders have compensated for declining state support by increasing the portion of their revenue from tuition (Heller, 2001a). As shown in Figure 3.1, over the 20-year period, tuition has increased from about 13 per cent of revenue at four-year public colleges to about 19 per cent. During that same period, the revenue they derived from state governments declined from more than 45.6 per cent to 35.7 per cent. There are, however, other reasons for tuition inflation. Public college campuses now regularly provide students with services, programmes, and amenities that were unknown a generation ago (Hauptman, 1990). Technology costs have increased steadily, and employee health and benefit costs have experienced significant price increases (Mumper, 2001).

Figure 3.2: Average tuition and fees at public two-year colleges, enrolment weighted (US $)

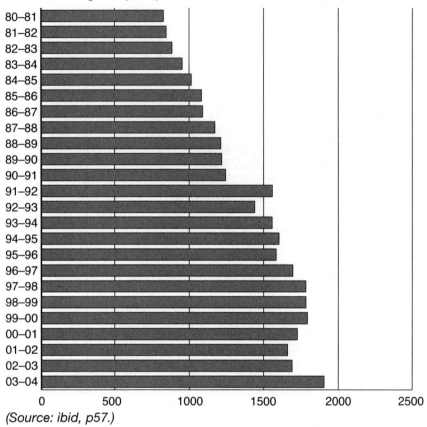

(Source: ibid, p57.)

Regardless of which causes are really driving the recent tuition inflation, there is every reason to expect that the trend will continue into the next decade. State budgets have deteriorated rapidly since 2000, forcing further cuts to public higher education.

Increased demand for new spending on Medicaid, law enforcement, and elementary and secondary education compete each year with higher education, drawing revenues away. Barring any unexpected changes in the revenue structure of state government, or the discovery of a reliable new revenue source by campus leaders, tuition inflation will only accelerate. Similarly, campuses are spending more, not less, on new programmes and services. In addition, technology and health costs continue to rise at rapid rates. This will force disadvantaged and low-

Figure 3.3: College participation rates by income quartile for dependent 18- to 24-year-olds

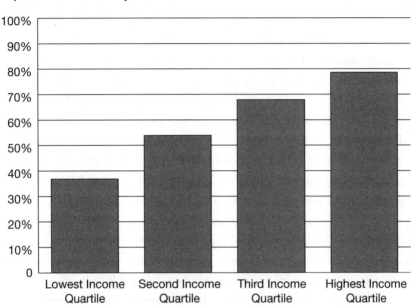

(Source: Mortenson, 2003b.)

income students to find ways to cover these ever rising prices if they do not want to be closed out of the economic rewards that college brings.

These patterns are more troubling since tuition increases have a disproportionate impact on low-income students (Heller, 1999). Kane (1995) has made a series of studies examining the link between rising prices and college participation. This research suggests that as the net price of higher education increases, the participation rates for low-income students declines. This is true even when both tuition and overall enrolments are rising. Looking at Massachusetts, which had especially dramatic increases in tuition in the 1980s and 1990s, he found that the gap between upper- and lower-income enrolments increased as tuition increased. He concludes that a $1,000 increase in tuition at four-year public colleges reduces enrolment in that sector by 13.7 per cent for whites and 21.4 per cent for blacks (Kane, 1998).

The role of the Federal Government

Because state policy makers have been unable to keep tuition low, the role of the Federal Government has become even more important. The traditional federal role in increasing college access for low-income students was to provide a safety-net, ensuring that no qualified student is shut out of higher education. The centrepiece of this effort was the Pell Grant programme. Originally called the Basic Educational Opportunity Grant (BEOG), Pell was established in the Higher Education Act of 1965. In its original form, the BEOG was allocated directly to institutions, which were left free to determine who would be eligible for aid and how much each student would receive. But, with the 1972 amendments to the Higher Education Act, Congress created a national system of needs analysis in which each student applying for federal financial aid was subjected to a means test (Gladieux and Wolanin, 1976). The estimated price of tuition and living expenses at an institution, and the student's family income were used to determine eligibility for a federal grant, loan, or work-study assistance.

The Pell Grant was to provide the foundation funding that would ensure that the most needy would have substantial college support. In 1974, the first year it was awarded, the maximum Pell Grant (the one awarded to the most needy students), purchased 78 per cent of the annual cost of one year at an average-priced public college or university (College Board, 2001b). This went a long way towards removing price barriers for low-income students.

By almost all accounts, the newly targeted Pell Grant produced some dramatic results in the years after the first awards were given out. A meta-analysis of six econometric studies of the Pell Grant and college enrolment found that, as the programme existed in the late 1970s, it raised lower-income enrolment by between 20 and 40 per cent (Leslie and Brinkman, 1987). However, almost since its creation, Pell funding has badly lagged behind the pace of tuition inflation. Table 3.1 shows the problem. While the size of the maximum award has increased slowly, its purchasing power has steadily eroded. Today, the Pell Grant covers less than 40 per cent of the cost of a public four-year college.

Table 3.1: Maximum Pell Grant as per cent of average cost of attendance at a four-year public institution – selected years 1980–2002 (in constant 2002 dollars)

Year	Maximum Pell Grant (US$)	Average Pell Grant (US$)	Maximum Pell Grant as percent of average cost of attendance at a four-year public institution
1980	3,634	1,831	67.1
1985	3,471	2,114	54.2
1990	3,089	1,946	44.3
1995	2,724	1,764	34.7
2000	3,785	2,096	45.0
2002	4,000	2,415	40.3

This has left disadvantaged students with fewer and fewer grant resources to pay for rising college costs.

Beginning only a few years later, the direction of federal student aid policy began a steady change that would eventually transform it from a grant-based system into a loan-based system (Hearn, 1998). Congress created the guaranteed student loan programme, now called the Stafford Loan, in the Higher Education Act of 1965. While eligibility for these loans was also means-tested, they were available to students from higher-income groups than was the case with Pell Grants. Federal loan guarantees were originally intended to be a supplement to the centrepiece grant programme, but almost immediately the demand for loans exceeded expectations (Mumper, 1996). As early as 1975, the Federal Government awarded more student aid dollars in loans than it did in grants. However, the real explosion in student loans began with the enactment of the Middle Income Student Assistance Act in 1978. This removed the income eligibility requirements from the guaranteed student loan programme and allowed virtually all full-time students to take out a government guaranteed and subsidized loan. The result was an explosion of student borrowing and a parallel growth in the loan components of the student aid programmes. Between 1977 and 1981, the amount of student loans awarded increased from $4.2 billion to more than $13 billion (as measured in 2001 dollars) and the number of borrowers increased from 1 million to 3.2 million (Gillespie and Carlson, 1983).

In 1981, the Reagan Administration entered office determined to sharply reduce the size of the Federal Government's social spending. Large cuts were proposed for both the Pell Grant and the guaranteed loan programmes. While those efforts were not successful at reducing overall student aid spending, they did slow the growth of the loan programmes and restore an income cap for student loan eligibility, albeit at a higher level than it had been in 1978. But after the expansion, cutting back the student loan programme proved virtually impossible. Middle-income students and their families were beginning to feel the effects of the tuition inflation discussed previously. They saw student loans as a simple, and subsidised, way to cover their rising costs. This set off an unprecedented expansion in student borrowing. The $13 billion awarded in student loan aid in 1980 tripled to $40 billion in 1999 (College Board, 2001b). During that same time period, total federal grant spending went from about $18 million to $27 million, an increase of only 33 per cent.

The 20 years of growth in federal student loans and their growing cost to the Federal Treasury are undoubtedly a part of the reason for the decline in the Pell Grant programme over the same period. While Congress was spending more each year on students, they were steadily shifting subsidies away from the most needy to often considerably less needy middle-income students. The increase in student borrowing, and subsequent loan debt, among low-income students presented another important concern. Low-income students do not benefit from loans in the same way as do middle-income students. Fossey (1998) describes the problem this way:

> Not all students who take out student loans are benefited. Many – low-income students, single parents, and minority individuals, in particular – are defaulting. And many more who do not default are heavily burdened by their student loan commitments. Without any question, a certain portion of students see the quality of their lives decline rather than improve because they borrowed money to finance their education. (p. 4)

The role of public college admissions practices

Public college admissions procedures played a central role by advancing the cause of equal opportunity. The Civil Rights Act of 1964 established a national policy of non-discrimination that was broadly understood to involve the elimination of overt discrimination and the adoption of colour blind practices (Sindler, 1987, p. 12). However, within a short time of its enactment, this early view of non-discrimination was judged by many to be too limited to achieve the desired results. In their view, additional and special efforts were needed to promote equal opportunity for minority groups. The result was that a number of varied 'something more' procedures were put into place by campus leaders. These came to be known as affirmative admissions policies. Such procedures became common in college admissions through the 1970s.

These admissions practices were challenged many times in court on the grounds that 'something more' amounted to an unfair advantage and that college admissions should be race-neutral. In 1978, the US Supreme Court addressed this controversy in the case of Allan Bakke v. Regents of the University of California. In its ruling, the Court held that colleges and universities can consider race as a factor in determining admission, but that they cannot establish a fixed quota of student slots assigned on the basis of race. This ruling allowed public universities to continue to consider race as a 'plus factor' in an effort to ensure the campus maintained campus diversity.

This all changed in 1996, when the US Fifth Circuit Court issued their decision in Hopwood v. Texas. The Court ruled that colleges, in this case a law school, cannot 'give any consideration to race or ethnicity . . . for the purposes of achieving a diverse student body.' The US Supreme Court refused to hear the case on appeal and the ruling stood. The State of Texas interpreted the decision as applying to admission at all public colleges and universities and to the allocation of scholarships (Hurtato and Cade, 2001). At about the same time, the voters of the State of California passed Proposition 209 which, among other things, prohibited the granting of preferential treatment to any individual on the basis of race, sex, colour, ethnicity, or national origin in admission to the state's institutions of higher education. A wave of race-blind admissions policies quickly replaced the long-standing affirmative admissions policies.

This change in admissions practices has resulted in a precipitous drop in the number of minority students admitted to the most selective institutions in those states. For example, resident freshman enrolment at the University of California dropped from 7.8 per cent in autumn 1997 to 3.7 per cent only one year later (Pusser, 2001, p. 138). In other cases, campuses responded to these trends by resorting to greater reliance on standardised tests in admissions decisions. Orfield (1998) notes that: 'Once affirmative action was stripped away . . . the consequences of ranking applicants by standardized tests became much more obvious.'. He goes on:

> under the new rules, there have been devastating declines in the admission of underrepresented minority students. A recent study suggests that even without the use of standardized tests, differences in grades alone would produce major drops in the enrollment of black and Latino students. (p.7)

These actions compound the impact of the income and price trends discussed earlier. Minority students may now find it more difficult to gain admission to their institution of choice, even if they are able to overcome the financial barriers.

The reasons for the redesign

If the Great Society Design was working so well throughout the 1970s, why was it replaced? No single factor or event was responsible. It occurred through countless amendments, changes in regulations, court decisions, appropriations bills, and new initiatives. But three forces seem to clearly have played important roles. Most obviously, the policy makers who designed the Great Society approach were replaced with a new generation of leaders who did not support the goals or values of the policies. Indeed, by the 1990s, it was difficult to find more than a handful of national policy makers who remained vocal supporters of the Great Society. But despite these changes, the goal of improving college access for the disadvantaged remained widely popular. Presidential and congressional candidates from both parties extolled the importance of college access and lamented the trends in college participation.

A second reason for the transformation is an almost natural result of tinkering with the policy. The Great Society Design focused on targeting subsidies to the most needy students. Over time, however, there is pressure to spread those subsidies up the income ladder to less needy students. This is because targeting benefits to the disadvantaged does not generate the political support that follows spreading subsidies to the middle- and upper-income earners. In 1978, for example, Congress bowed to public pressure and, in the Middle Income Student Assistance Act, opened up eligibility to subsidised loans to students from all income groups. These changes were often presented as ways to make the benefits of these valuable programmes available to an even wider group of students. In the 1980s, eligibility for the Title IV programmes was changed such that families with higher incomes could qualify for Pell Grants. As tuition spiralled upwards in the 1980s and 1990s, the pressure on Congress to further spread those subsidies intensified. It responded by developing a new set of tax credits and deductions that directly subsidised middle- and upper-income students. While none of these initiatives directly challenged the targeted Great Society Design, they redistributed an ever larger percentage of the funds available for college support away from the most needy.

There was also a third factor driving the transformation in college access policy. This was a fundamental change in the approach many policy makers took to designing social policy. The view that government subsidies should be carefully targeted to the most disadvantaged (the Great Society view) was replaced with a 'universalist' view that subsidies should be spread widely across social and economic groups. During the 1970s and 1980s, the conventional wisdom was that government subsidies should be carefully targeted to the most disadvantaged. Indeed, targeting benefits by means-tests and resource-based eligibility requirements became the hallmark of the Great Society initiatives. Eligibility for food stamps, Medicaid, SSI, subsidised housing, and Pell Grants are all need-based. Anti-poverty policies of this era are almost synonymous with targeted public assistance.

The logic of the targeted design is that since public funds will always be limited, targeting produces the most efficient allocation. More of the benefits reach those who need them the most. In this view, social problems are complex and persistent, and fighting them requires us to maximise our resources. Making progress towards reducing crime or poverty or improving school performance usually requires a multi-faceted approach which attacks different parts of the problem simultaneously. In *Within Our Reach* (1988), for example, Lisbeth Schorr lays out a comprehensive approach to poverty reduction that targets multiple types of aid to those in the highest-risk groups. This type of intensive intervention would be impossibly expensive unless it was carefully targeted to the most needy.

Beginning in the 1990s, these conventional policy designs began to come under sharp criticism. Everyone agrees that, other things being equal, the more effectively a policy discriminates between beneficiaries, the greater its potential impact on the targeted population.

But other things are rarely equal. Critics argue that fine targeting of benefits comes at an important cost to the poor. Targeting produces higher administrative costs. But most importantly, critics argue that targeted programmes cannot attract the broad political support necessary to sustain them over long periods of time. The most compelling presentation of this view was made by William Julius Wilson in *The Truly Disadvantaged* (1987). Wilson argues that government programmes that target benefits narrowly to the most needy are not likely to succeed because they cannot maintain the support of a sufficient number of middle- and upper-income voters to ensure the programme's long-term political viability. In a section of the book titled 'The Hidden Agenda: From Group Specific to Universal Programs of Reform,' Wilson argues that social programmes should be designed and presented as offering benefits to the broadest possible constituency. As the universal programmes draw support from the wide population, the benefits going to the targeted group will likewise be supported and protected. Wilson sums up the argument in this way:

> Accordingly, the hidden agenda for liberal policy makers is to improve the life chances of the truly disadvantaged . . . by emphasizing programs to which the more advantaged groups of all races and class backgrounds can relate. (p. 155)

This universal position has been more fully developed by Theda Skocpol. In a series of detailed policy histories, she attempts to show that progressive social programmes can be popular among the American public, and those programmes can be politically viable over long periods of time. This can only be done, however, if they are designed to provide benefits to broad coalitions rather than narrowly targeted. In several different works she traces the development of the social programmes that provide benefit to Civil War veterans (1995), the Social Security program (1995), public education (2000), and the GI Bill (1992). In each of these cases, she illustrates how a universal design proved essential in maintaining their support in difficult budgetary times. In other cases, she provides detailed reviews of the failure of initiatives in which benefits are more targeted, including the mother's pension programmes of the early 1900s (1992), many of the Great Society initiatives (2000, pp. 43–58), and the failure of the Clinton health care plan (1997).

> Historically, Americans have been perfectly happy to benefit from federal government spending, and even pay higher taxes to finance spending that is generous and benefits more privileged groups and citizens and not just the poor. Such benefits are especially appealing if they flow in administratively streamlined and relatively automatic ways. (Skocpol, 1997a, p. 167)

In *The Missing Middle* (Skocpol, 2000), she outlines the formula for a successful social policy. A central element of this formula is the policy design.

> Successful social programs have built bridges between more and less privileged Americans, bringing people together – as worthy beneficiaries and contributing citizens – across lines of class, race, and region. (p. 30)

Additional evidence for this universal strategy is found in comparing the designs of the American and Western European style welfare systems. Skocpol (1995) argues that the European social insurance systems have been more stable than the American public assistance model because they provide substantial benefits to middle- and upper-income families as well as to the poor (pp. 7–136). The reason that the American system of public assistance has been so vulnerable to cutbacks, and its recipients so easily marginalised, is that their targeted design isolates the poor from the non-poor. On the other hand, the European model of extended social insurance benefits is sustainable precisely because it is so large. Seen in this way, the problem with developing and sustaining progressive policies in the USA is not that the programmes are too big and expensive, but that they are not ambitious enough to be sustained.

It is important not to draw the distinction between the two design strategies too sharply. Even those who are the most critical of the universalist approach do not deny that the approach has merit. Rather they argue that it ignores budgetary realities and that it is unrealistic to expect the construction of vast new social programmes providing benefits for large portions of the population. The federal and state governments are continually searching for ways to cut spending and to curb expensive new initiatives. At the same time, the public demand for services inevitably outstrips the available resources. In this context, elected officials are understandably hesitant to raise taxes, even for those programmes that have broad popular support. Greenstein puts it this way:

> Advocates of universal programs frequently contend that if a program will benefit the entire population, the public may accept a tax increase. In a nation with a historic aversion to the size of government and the level of taxation found in Western Europe, the degree to which additional resources can be raised for new universal programs is likely to be limited. (p. 454)

Lacking the resources to generate new universal programmes, and recognising that even in good times the next budget crisis is only a few years away, targeting seems to some to provide the only realistic option. Indeed, in this budgetary context, too great an emphasis on costly universal programmes will inevitably result in too few resources being directed to those at the bottom of the economic ladder (Greenstein, 1991, p. 457).

The redesign of college access policy

Whether or not this was a causal factor, public policies to increase college access were redesigned in the 1980s and 1990s in ways consistent with the universalist approach. The elements of the Great Society Design that targeted benefits to the most needy were eliminated and under-funded, and the targeting mechanisms were relaxed. At the same time those programmes that spread subsidies broadly across all economic groups were expanded and new programmes were developed that targeted subsidies directly to middle income and even affluent students. As early as 1990, Thomas Mortenson recognised the trans-formation that was under way in college access policy. He describes it this way:

> Since 1978, federal, state, and institutional student financial aid developments have consistently expanded programs, eligibility, and benefits for students from middle and affluent family income backgrounds. Moreover, often these enhancements have been financed by shifting money previously designated for low income students to those higher family income students. (p. 3)

Throughout the 1980s, federal aid shifted from grants to loans. The Pell Grant formula was changed to extend eligibility well into the middle income group. The elimination of Social Security survivors' benefits for college hurt primarily low-income students. State universities raised their admissions standards. This excluded many lower-income students and preserved the large subsidies for middle- and upper-income students. Moreover, the development of pre-paid tuition and savings plans benefit only those who have discretionary money to save for college.

This pattern accelerated in the 1990s. In the face of rising tuition and the limited availability of direct grants, state and federal policy makers undertook a major effort to overhaul the way the governments finance higher education. They did not eliminate the existing programmes. Rather, they constructed a new, parallel system of student support based on very different principles. These new programmes represent the most fundamental change in the nation's higher education policy since the Great Society. Over the next few decades, this 'new generation' of programmes is poised to replace the traditional framework as the foundation of higher education finance. This will not happen through a direct replacement, but a slower process in which all new funds are directed to the new generation programmes and the value of the traditional programmes continues to erode. These new programmes are designed to make college more affordable to middle- and upper-income students. This is a noble goal, but in this case, realising it seems likely to come at the cost of access for the lower-income students. The programmes that best exemplify this new approach to college finance are the federal HOPE scholarship and Lifelong Learning tax credit and the various state level merit scholarship programmes modelled after Georgia's HOPE scholarship.[1]

The Taxpayer Relief Act of 1997 created a number of new programmes designed to help families pay for college. These included the federal HOPE Scholarship, the Lifetime Learning credit, a student loan interest deduction, and an expansion of education IRAs (Wolanin, 2001). The HOPE scholarship and Lifelong Learning credit are by far the largest of the initiatives, allowing students to obtain credits that reduce their federal tax liability. They are designed to provide relief for those students who are already going to college rather than providing an incentive for others to attend. Also, as shown in Table 3.2, the HOPE scholarship and Lifelong Learning credit were not designed to target benefits to the most needy. Instead:

> These two new programs are targeted toward students and families who generally are not eligible for need based grants but still need financial assistance to meet all of their expenses. The tax credit programs include

> income caps to prevent upper income students from qualifying for benefits while providing relief to middle income students. But they do relatively little to aid low income students, most of whom have no tax liability, and, therefore will not be eligible for the credit. (Hoblitzell and Smith, 2001, pp. 1–2)

These tax credits involve no direct payment to students. Deductions are made from a family's tax liability and it is assumed that those dollars saved will be used for educational expenses. Moreover, tax credits do not occur until taxes are filed, up to 18 months later. Students must pay college costs from other sources and await reimbursement.

These programmes carry a substantial cost, but it must be measured in foregone revenues rather than direct expenditures. The estimated cost of these new higher education tax credit programmes is $41 billion over the first five years (Kane, 1999, p. 43). This is already roughly the same size as the Pell Grant programme, and it is almost certain to grow during the next decade as more eligible students use the tax credits and institutions begin to set prices so that students can take full advantage of the programme benefits.

The vast majority of these tax credits go to middle- and upper-middle-income students. Disadvantaged families who pay little or no tax are less likely to be aware of the tax credit and more likely to attend lower-priced community colleges. Table 3.2 shows that the benefits of the tax credit are directed toward families with taxable annual incomes between $40,000 and $80,000. This is far above the eligibility for the Pell Grant that usually is awarded to only those with taxable incomes below $40,000. Thus, the HOPE credit represents a new type of targeting in which the most needy are left out entirely and awards are carefully targeted to the politically powerful middle-income families (Wolanin, 2001). The result is a not-so-subtle redistribution of benefits to families higher up the income ladder. In annual appropriations battles, the funds for Pell Grants must come out of federal revenues that have already been reduced by revenues lost to the HOPE credits. Given these patterns, it seems certain that the Federal Government will continue to spend more on these tax expenditure programmes (as well as the various student loan programmes) and it will have little positive

Table 3.2: Estimated value of HOPE tax credits by taxable income

Taxable income (US $)	HOPE tax credit at public four-year colleges (US $)	HOPE tax credit at public two-year colleges (US $)
10,000	0	0
20,000	0	0
30,000	550	550
40,000	1,500	1,250
50,000	1,500	1,250
60,000	1,500	1,250
70,000	1,500	1,250
80,000	1,500	1,250
90,000	750	625
10,000	0	0

(Source: Wolanin, 2001.)

impact on the college access available to disadvantaged students and their families.

State governments also made policy changes in the 1990s to address the problem of rising college costs. The fastest-growing state initiatives in this regard are merit scholarships modelled on the popular HOPE scholarship program in Georgia. These merit programmes offer full or partial scholarships to all graduates of a state high school who earn a specified GPA and attend an in-state public college or university. On its face, such programmes seem like an ideal way for states to encourage and reward academic achievement without regard for the student's racial or economic status. In practice however, the early evidence is that, like the federal tax credits, these merit aid programmes direct a large portion of their funds to middle- and upper-income students. Lower- income students are less likely to meet the minimum GPA, less likely to maintain it through college, and more likely to attend less expensive institutions.

Since 1990, thirteen states have established new merit scholarship programmes and eight more operate programmes that have a merit component (NASSGAP, 2004). While these programmes vary in their structure, funding source, and eligibility criteria, all ignore the student's family income. The dollar growth of these merit programmes is especially noteworthy.

At the state level, new grant aid has shifted steadily in favor of merit based aid and against need based aid. Since 1993, funding of merit programs has increased by 336 percent in real dollars. During the same time period, funding for need- based financial aid programs had increased only 88 percent, which reflects the broad political appeal and support for these programs. (ACSFA, 2001 p. 8)

Today, more than $900 million, or 23 per cent of total state grants, are awarded as merit scholarships, up from 10 per cent in 1991 (NASSGAP, 2004). While these merit scholarship programmes seem to be designed to appeal to all families, only those students who meet the requisite grade or test requirements earn the award. In most programmes, the student must also maintain a predetermined GPA to keep the scholarship. In practice this has meant that a far higher percentage of upper- and middle-income students receive the award. Lower-income and minority students, who often come from lower-performing high schools, receive these scholarships in much smaller percentages.

A study of Florida's Bright Futures merit scholarship programme by Heller and Rasmussen (2001) shows the desperate impact the award structure has by race. The Bright Futures programme was created in 1997 and is now the second largest state-run merit programme. Initial awards cover 75 per cent of tuition and fees at an in-state public college or a comparable amount at a private institution. To qualify, students must earn a 1280 on the SAT or 28 on the ACT. Eligible students who have completed 75 hours of public service can receive 100 per cent of tuition and fees. Students must maintain a 3.0 GPA while in college to retain the award.

In analysing participation in the programme, Heller found that whites were much more likely to win a Bright Futures scholarship. In 1998, about 61 per cent of Florida's high school graduates were white. But they received more than 76 per cent of the scholarships. African-Americans and Hispanics constitute 21 and 14 per cent of the graduates respectively. Yet, African-Americans receive only 7.5 per cent of the scholarships while Hispanics receive 10 per cent. There is no reason to believe that similar differences in the race and income levels of recipients would not be found in every state merit scholarship programme.

In his testimony before the Advisory Committee on Student Financial Assistance, Heller lamented this trend.

> There is no question that the focus of state scholarship programs is moving away from serving needy students. While the bulk of the state dollars spent for financial aid is still in need-based programs, virtually all of the new initiatives have been geared towards merit scholarship programs. And evidence is becoming available that merit scholarship programs do little to serve needy students, but rather, are addressed at the political interests of middle and upper income students and their families. (Heller, 2001b, p.3)

This emergence of this new generation of federal and state student aid programmes has utterly undermined the goal of equal opportunity that characterised the earlier programmes. These are explicitly not need-based programmes. Instead, they are designed to make higher education more affordable to middle- and even upper-income families. There is substantial evidence that these programmes are creating a future in which government spending on student aid is ever increasing and yet the access available to lower-income students is ever diminishing. Indeed, the politics of these new generation programmes almost guarantees that they will expand. As college prices rise, there will be enormous pressure on policy makers to ensure that the value of the tax credits keeps pace with those increases. Similarly, state merit scholarship programmes will cost states more each year as tuition increases, and this will bring enormous pressure to maintain the programmes in their present structure. One commentator described it this way:

> The biggest problem with the scholarships may be simply that the public loves them too much. College officials and lawmakers alike complain that the merit programs have become so popular that they are impossible to change. For some state policy makers, the scholarships are becoming to middle-class parents what Social Security is to an older generation. (Selingo, 2001 p. A20)

Table 3.3: Percentage distribution of current fund revenue at four-year public degree granting institutions by source

Type of revenue	1980	1985	1990	1995	2000
Tuition and fees	12.9	14.5	16.1	18.8	18.9
Federal government	12.8	10.5	10.3	11.1	10.6
State government	45.6	45.0	40.3	35.8	35.7
Local government	3.8	3.6	3.7	4.1	3.8
Private gifts	2.5	3.2	3.8	4.1	4.5
Endowment income	0.5	0.6	0.5	0.6	0.6
Sales and services	19.6	20.0	22.7	22.2	22.3
Other	2.4	2.6	2.6	3.3	3.7

(Source: Mortenson, 2003b.)

Bruce Manlett, executive director of the New Mexico Commission on Higher Education, echoed these concerns with their merit programme when he said, 'If it isn't an entitlement yet, in folks' minds then it is getting pretty close' (in Selingo, 2001, p. A21). Georgia State Representative Charlie Barnes put it this way: 'It's less painful to jump off a cliff than to change HOPE' (in Selingo, 2001, p. A20).

As the tax credit programmes are more widely understood and institutionalised, and the merit scholarship model migrates to other states, their cost will mushroom. It is almost inevitable that they will attract a larger and larger portion of government spending on higher education which will, in turn, push tuition up and grant support down. Any attempt to restrain the growth of these new-generation programmes will mobilise their vast numbers of middle-income supporters. Breaking that spiral will prove even more difficult as a generation of middle- and upper-income families build their children's college funds on the assumption that these benefits will always be there.

Twenty years of policy change: goal substitution, subsidy creep, and diminished access

Since the development of the Great Society Design, the state and federal programmes intended to improve college access have been transformed. Policies that had originally been designed to address the problem of access for the disadvantaged morphed into programmes to address the very different problem of middle-income affordability. This substitution changed the basic rationale of the programmes. Evidence of this substitution can be seen most clearly in the language used by policy makers as they speak about student aid. As Heller (2001a), summarises the shift:

> When you listen to the language used in discussions of state scholarships by state legislators, as well as by governors, you can see an almost exclusive focus on phrases like 'middle-class affordability', encouraging academic achievement' and 'rewarding hard work.' Words like 'promoting access' 'helping needy students,' or 'promoting equal opportunity' are entirely missing from the debate. (p. 3)

Through more than 20 years of adjustments, revisions, and additions, policy makers have been able to satisfy the demands of middle-income families and still appear to continue to support the programme goal of increasing college access for low-income students. While this was driven by pressure from middle-income families, it was also encouraged by a new approach to policy design which advocates universal rather than targeted programmes. The result has been that a system built on low tuition and need-based grants was replaced with one of loans, tax credits, and merit scholarships. As policy makers shifted subsidies away from the lowest-income students, the real price of public higher education increased rapidly for the most needy. Table 3.4, taken from a recent study by the Advisory Committee on Student Financial Assistance (2002), shows that low-income, college-qualified high school graduates now face an annual unmet need of $3,800 in expenses at a four-year public college not covered by student aid. This creates a financial barrier that prevents as many as 48 per cent of college-qualified low-income high school graduates from attending a four-year college within two years of graduation. That translates into a national total of more than 400,000 college-qualified students who are unable to attend a four-year college this year. The committee described the consequences of these trends this way:

> While the considerable investment in need-based student aid over the

Table 3.4: Average annual unmet need facing high school
graduates by family income and type of college

Public two-year college

Annual family income	Annual unmet need
Less than $25,000/year	$3,200
$25,000-$50,000/year	$2,700
$50,000-$75,000/year	$600
More than $75,000/year	$100

Public four-year college

Annual family income	Annual unmet need
Less than $25,000/year	$38,00
$25,000-$50,000/year	$3,000
$50,000-$75,000/year	$1,500
More than $75,000/year	$400

(Source: Advisory Committee on Student Financial Assistance, 2002.)

> last three decades has modestly improved postsecondary participation,
> persistence, and completion rates of low-income youth, the shift in policy
> priorities at all levels away from access has caused a steep rise in unmet
> need. Thus, low-income participation and persistence rates continue to
> lag well behind those of middle- and upper-income youth. Each year, yet
> another cohort of low-income youth – academically prepared to attend
> postsecondary education full time – confronts significant financial barriers
> making that aspiration nearly impossible. (ACSFA, 2001, p. 10)

The same conclusion can be drawn about the entire effort to ensure
college access for disadvantaged students. Despite considerable
investment, things are no better, and perhaps worse, than they were 25
years ago.

One final consequence of the redesign of college access policy is the
increasing economic segregation of higher education. Low-income
students, as measured by Pell Grant eligibility, are increasingly pushed
towards two-year public colleges. Those low-income students who opt
for a four-year public college are usually segregated into open-door,
four-year institutions. The reverse is true for upper-income and wealthy
students, who disproportionately attend the most selective four-year

institutions in the USA. In fact, in 1980, 60 per cent of Pell Grant recipients attended a public, four-year institution, while 40 per cent attended a two-year institution. In 2002, however, only 44.7 per cent of Pell Grant recipients attended a public, four-year institution, while 55.3 per cent attended a two-year institution (Mortenson, 2003b). This growing economic segregation of American higher education has been the direct result of federal, state, and institutional policies. As shown in Figure 3.3, the cumulative effect of these policies has resulted in the sorting and redistribution of higher education according to economic class (Mortenson, 2003b). As a result, higher education today often serves to reinforce the existing patterns of stratification and exacerbate the nation's widening income gap. This role is precisely the opposite of the one it played a generation ago.

Notes

1 The Federal Hope Scholarship was loosely based on the Georgia program. While the federal program operates differently, it retains the same name given to Georgia's program by then-Governor Zell Miller.

References

ACSFA (2001) *Access Denied: restoring the nation's commitment to equal educational opportunity*. Washington DC: Advisory Committee on Student Financial Assistance.

ACFSA (2002) *Empty Promises: the myth of college access in America*. Washington DC: Advisory Committee on Student Financial Assistance.

Boehner, J. A. and McKeon, H. P. (2003) *The College Cost Crisis: a congressional analysis of college costs and implications for America's higher education system*. Washington, DC: US Congress.

Carnevale, A. and Fry, R. (2000) *Crossing the Great Divide: can we achieve equity when Generation Y goes to college?* Princeton NJ: Educational Testing Service.

College Board (2001a) *Trends in College Pricing*. Washington DC: College Board.

College Board (2001b). *Trends in Student Aid*. Washington DC: College Board.

Fossey, R. (1998) Introduction in R. Fossey and M. Bateman (eds), *Condemning Students to Debt: College loans and public policy*. New York: Teachers College Press.

Gillespie, D. and Carlson, N. (1983) *Trends in student aid: 1963–1993*. Washington DC: College Board.

Gladieux, L. and Wolanin, T. (1976) *Congress and the Colleges*. Lexington MA: Lexington Books.

Greenstein, R. (1991) Universal and targeted approaches to relieving poverty: An alternative view. In C. Jenks and P. Peterson (eds), *The Urban Underclass*, pp. 437–59. Washington DC: Brookings Institution.

Hauptman, A. (1990) *The College Tuition Spiral*. Washington DC: The American Council on Education.

Hearn, J. (1998) The Growing Loan Orientation of Federal Financial Aid Policy: A historical perspective. In R. Fossey and M. Bateman (eds), *Condemning Students to Debt: College loans and public policy*, pp. 47–75. New York: Teachers College Press.

Heller, D. (1999) 'The Effects of Tuition and State Financial Aid on Public College Enrollment', *Review of Higher Education*, Vol. 23, No 1, pp. 65–90.

Heller, D. and Rasmussen, C. (2001) *Merit Scholarships: Evidence from two states*. Unpublished manuscript.

Heller, D. (2001a) Trends in the Affordability of Public Colleges and Universities: The Contradiction of Increasing Prices and Increasing enrollment. In D. Heller (ed.), *The States and Public Higher Education Policy: Affordability, access, and accountability*, pp. 11–38. Baltimore: Johns Hopkins Press.

Heller, D. (2001b) Remarks before the Advisory Committee on Student Financial Assistance in response to *Access Denied*. February 20, 2001, Washington DC.

Hoblitzell, B. and Smith, T. (2001) *Hope Works: Student use of education tax credits*. Indianapolis: Lumina Foundation New Agenda Series.

Hurtado, C. and Cade, H. W. (2001) Time for Retreat or Renewal? Perspectives on the effects of Hopwood on campus. In D. Heller (ed.), *The States and Public Higher Education Policy: Affordability, access, and accountability*, pp. 100–20. Baltimore: Johns Hopkins Press.

Jenks, C. (1971) Social Stratification in Higher Education. In M. D. Orwig (ed.), *Financing Higher Education: Alternatives for the federal government*, pp. 71–115. Iowa City, IA: American College Testing Program.

Kane, T. (1995) Rising Public College Tuition and College Entry: How well do public subsidies promote access to college? National Bureau of Economic Research Working Paper No. 5164.

Kane, T. (1998) *Taking Stock at the End of Three Decades of Federal Financial Aid*. Unpublished manuscript.

Kane, T. (1999) *The Price of Admission: Rethinking how Americans pay for college*. Washington DC: Brookings Institution.

King, J. (2000) *Status Report on the Pell Grant Program*. Washington DC: American Council on Education.

Leslie, L. and Brinkman, P. (1987) 'Student Price Response in Higher Education', *Journal of Higher Education*, Vol. 58, No 2, pp. 181–204.

McPherson, M. and Schapiro, M. O. (1999) *Reinforcing Stratification in American Higher Education: Some disturbing trends*. Stanford CA: National Center for Postsecondary Improvement, Stanford University.

Mortenson, T. (1990) *Reallocation of Financial Aid from Poor to Middle Income and More Affluent Students – 1978 to 1990*. Iowa City: American ACT Reports.

Mortenson, T. (2001) 'College Participation by Family Income, Gender, and Race/Ethnicity for Dependent 18–24 year olds: 1996–2000', *Postsecondary Education Opportunity*, Vol. 144, No. 1.

Mortenson, T. (2003) *Pell Grant Students in Undergraduate Enrollments by Institutional Type and Control 1992–93 to 2001–02.* In Postsecondary Education Opportunity, December 2003, pp. 1–16.

Mumper, M. (2001) The Paradox of College Prices: Five Stories With No Clear Lesson. In D. Heller (ed.), *The States and Public Higher Education Policy: Affordability, access, and accountability*, pp. 11–38. Baltimore: Johns Hopkins Press.

Mumper, M. (1996) *Removing College Price Barriers: What government has done and why it hasn't worked.* Albany NY: SUNY Press.

NASSGAP (2004) http://nassgap.org/researchsurveys/default.htm

National Commission on the Costs of Higher Education (1999) *Straight Talk About College Costs and Prices.* Washington DC: American Council on Education.

Orfield, G. (1998) Campus Restratification and its Alternatives. In G. Orfield and E. Miller (eds), *Chilling Admissions*. Cambridge MA: Harvard Educational Publishing Group.

Pusser, B. (2001) The Contemporary Politics of Access Policy: California after Proposition 209. In D. Heller (ed.), *The States and Public Higher Education Policy: Affordability, access, and accountability*, pp. 121–50. Baltimore: Johns Hopkins Press.

Schorr, L. (1988) *Within our Reach: Breaking the cycle of disadvantage.* New York: Doubleday Dell.

Selingo, J. (2001) 'Questioning the Merit of Merit Scholarships', *Chronicle of Higher Education*, January 19, 2001, pp. A20–A22.

Sindler, A. (1978) *Bakke, DeFunis, and Minority Admissions*. New York: Longman Publishing.

Skocpol, T. (1992) *Protecting Soldiers and Mothers: The political origins of social policy in America*. Cambridge, MA: Harvard University Press.

Skocpol, T. (1995) *Social Policy in the United States: Future possibilities in historical perspective*. Princeton NJ: Princeton University Press.

Skocpol, T. (1997a) *Boomerang: Health care reform and the turn against government*. New York: Norton.

Skocpol, T. (1997b) 'The G.I. Bill and Social Policy, Past and Future', *Social Philosophy and Policy*, Vol. 14, No 2, pp. 95–115.

Skocpol, T. (2000) *The Missing Middle*. New York: Norton.

Wilson, W. J. (1987) *The Truly Disadvantaged: The inner city, the underclass, and public policy*. Chicago: University of Chicago Press.

Wolanin, T. (2001) *Rhetoric and Reality: Effects and consequences of the HOPE scholarship*. Washington DC: Institute for Higher Education Policy.

Chapter 4

English higher education and near universal access: the college contribution

Gareth Parry

Introduction

In recent years, those institutions in England called 'further education colleges' have been assigned a prominent role in the future expansion of higher education. Although part of a long tradition of local, vocational and short cycle higher education, the place of the colleges in or around the English system of higher education has never been entirely clear. On the one hand, higher education has been a small fraction of the work of most colleges, with the majority of their academic, vocational and general programmes offered at the upper secondary and foundation levels. On the other, their higher education has been administered and funded through arrangements different from those applied to other courses. This duality and ambiguity has continued to the present day, being reinforced rather than challenged by the shift to mass higher education and now highlighted by policies that enlist colleges in the drive to wider participation and near universal access by the end of the decade.

In this paper, the changing nature and context for the college contribution to higher education in England is traced over the last 20 years. It was during this period that the English system made its decisive transition to mass higher education and, after a pause in the middle of the 1990s, embarked on a phase of renewed expansion. In reviewing this history, comparison is made of the growth trajectories displayed by the four countries in the United Kingdom to suggest that England was distinctive in the scale, shape and complexity of its passage from an extended elite to a mass system of higher education. The character of this achievement in England, it is argued, exercised an important influence on how colleges were expected to accomplish their revived and enhanced remit for higher education. By way of conclusion, questions are raised about the identity and sustainability of college-based higher education, including its capacity to address the multiple demands placed on it by the State and its agencies.

Three cautionary remarks need to be made at the outset. First, in this account, the model of elite-mass-universal higher education sketched by Trow (1974) is employed as a broad framework to interpret the development of tertiary arrangements in England. Similarly, the quantitative markers of the transition from one phase to another are adopted as a convenient heuristic. In the original model, elite systems were those which enrolled up to 15 to 20 per cent of an age grade; mass systems enrolled up to 50 per cent of the age grade; and universal systems enrolled even larger numbers and proportions. The schema and its application to the British case have not escaped criticism (Scott, 1995), although some of this is attached to the predictive elements in the model and 'the normative judgements which come so easily to the transatlantic pen' (Trow, 1989). Whatever the imputed weaknesses, its value here is to focus analytical attention on the relationship between higher education and other parts of the post-secondary system.

Secondly, the sources of data on higher education in further education colleges are more restricted and less reliable than for institutions of higher education, especially after new and separate data collection systems were introduced for the higher education and further education sectors. This is particularly so in England where colleges deliver, through franchise arrangements, a significant number of higher education courses on behalf of higher education establishments. Information on these programmes and their students is not captured in official sources, although derived statistics have been produced in the last few years.

Thirdly, these same colleges also provide courses that lead to vocational qualifications at the higher levels but which are not conventionally described as higher education. In the English system, an administrative definition of higher education has prevailed, with those courses above the A-level qualification (and its equivalents) regarded as higher education. At present, this separation is reflected in the existence of two national qualifications frameworks: one for higher education, specifying qualifications at five levels from certificates through to doctorates; and the other for qualifications below higher education, from entry level through to level 3 (where A-level and advanced vocational qualifications are found). In future, a single unified framework will be adopted, with higher education starting at the same point as before, at level 4. For the purpose of this paper, vocational qualifications at the higher levels are included as higher education.

These preliminary remarks signal key features and issues associated with the emergence of dual structures for the organisation, funding and quality assurance of post-compulsory education and training in England. The dual arrangements that currently shape the conditions for higher education in further education colleges were the result of reform measures introduced at the beginning of the 1990s and again at the opening of the new century. Following the Further and Higher Education Act of 1992, the post-secondary phase was divided into two sectors: a higher education sector for all higher education institutions and a further education sector for all further education establishments, including sixth form colleges. Following the Learning and Skills Act of 2000, a new and larger post-16 sector replaced the further education sector. Within this expanded sector, the colleges remained the largest group of education providers.

Under these arrangements, colleges were funded and inspected for their further education by their own sector bodies. The funding and assessment for their higher education, however, was divided between the two sectors. After 1999, the funding council for the higher education sector assumed responsibility for the greater part of this provision, bringing all undergraduate and postgraduate provision under the quality assessment agency for higher education and leaving the new learning and skills sector with responsibility for an assortment of higher level vocational, professional and technical qualifications.

At present, about one in nine of all higher education students in England are taught in the learning and skills sector. These account for just five per cent of the four million or so students recruited to further education colleges. In the higher education sector, a small number of students are enrolled on non-higher education programmes funded by the Learning and Skills Council. These account for five per cent of the around one and a half million students registered at higher education establishments.

The difficulties and the many complexities involved in these arrangements are outlined in the second half of this account. The background to these changes, and the contribution of the colleges to the rapid growth of higher education that began at the end of the 1980s, are discussed in the sections that follow. Both for the early years and the contemporary period, the history of non-university higher education is reported more fully for the polytechnics and the colleges of higher education (Matterson, 1981; Locke, Pratt and Burgess, 1985; Pratt, 1997) than for the colleges of further education (Cantor and Roberts, 1986; Cantor, Roberts and Pratley, 1995). In modern works on further education, there is usually a brief or passing reference to higher education in the college sector (Smithers and Robinson, 2000; Hyland and Merrill, 2003). Only in recent years have studies appeared which examine the policy and sector history of college-based higher education (Parry and Thompson, 2002; Parry, 2003).

Further education colleges: a third tier of local authority higher education

Prior to the 1992 Act which established further education colleges as independent corporations in their own college sector, these 300 or so institutions were owned and controlled by local government and funded through the local education authorities. Together with the 29 polytechnics and the 70 or more colleges of higher education, most of which were also local authority establishments before their incorporation under the Education Reform Act of 1988, they comprised the three main 'tiers' of public sector higher education. On the other side of the binary line, the 'autonomous' sector of self-governing universities was funded by central government, through grants allocated by an intermediary body. Unlike the universities which were legally empowered to award their own degrees, the higher education provided by the polytechnics, the colleges of higher education and the third tier of further education colleges were subject to approval, validation and inspection by external bodies.

The three sets of public sector institutions were, in turn, part of a larger system of further education that included adult education institutes and centres. While the polytechnics and higher education colleges offered mainly 'advanced' further education (as higher education was styled in the local authority system) most of the students in the colleges of further education were enrolled on courses of 'non-advanced' further education. Given the dominance of this level of provision in the colleges, most had quite small amounts of higher education; and some had no advanced work at all. In a sub-set of colleges, however, the advanced provision was a sizeable activity and contributed to their character as 'mixed economy' colleges. Over time, the polytechnics and, to a lesser extent, the colleges of higher education came to focus on higher education at the first degree and postgraduate levels. The colleges, on the other hand, were chiefly providers of short cycle vocational qualifications at the sub-degree levels (higher national diplomas and certificates), including courses leading to the examinations and awards made by various professional bodies.

In the system of further education, advanced work was funded at a higher level than non-advanced work and this was reflected in the pay and conditions of academic staff. A regional machinery existed for the approval of advanced courses and each local authority was able to charge to a central 'pool' its expenditure on advanced provision. Hence, for most administrative purposes, the key distinction was the level of work and not the type of institution. Except for the polytechnics, which owed their mission and title to decisions of central government, there was no national standard, expressed as a proportion or amount of advanced work, to distinguish between institutions of higher education and establishments of further education. This was evidenced in the variety of titles carried by colleges, each reflecting the different histories and circumstances of these institutions and their status as general or specialist colleges. Although no formal designations or demarcations were applied to the colleges, a difference was recognised between those predominantly involved with higher education and those – the largest in number – whose main concern was non-advanced work.

For colleges primarily engaged in non-advanced further education, their mission was the education of young people and adults beyond the compulsory stage, whether leading to academic and vocational qualifications at the upper secondary levels (including access to higher education), or involving programmes of general, liberal and basic education, or supplying employment and workforce training. By providing vocational and other qualifications not taught in schools, as well as part-time and full-time versions of courses available in secondary education, these establishments offered 'alternative routes' and 'second chance' opportunities for recent school-leavers and for adults returning to study.

The local access traditions and strong vocational profiles developed by several of these colleges were mirrored in their advanced further education courses. In addition to serving the education and training needs of the local and regional economy, including the specific requirements of major employers, their sub-degree vocational qualifications were commonly awarded by the national bodies for technician and business education. The same awarding bodies offered vocational qualifications at the lower levels, enabling colleges to provide 'staged access' to their own higher education. Furthermore, some of the large urban local authorities, such as in London and Manchester, used their responsibility for advanced and non-advanced further education to promote access and transfer between the colleges and polytechnics they controlled.

Since the 1970s, a decline in manufacturing industry had led to a proportional decline in apprenticeships and consequently in the day-release courses that colleges provided for employers. Not only were employers unable to release their employees but students on part-time courses of higher education – the dominant mode of study in the colleges – were not eligible for the mandatory grants that covered the costs of tuition and maintenance of full-time undergraduate students. At the same time, repeated attempts were made by central government to concentrate advanced work – full-time programmes in particular – in the larger and strongest institutions within the local authority system.

Nevertheless, the colleges of further education accounted for an estimated one in five of all higher education students in the non-university sector at the beginning of the 1980s. Standing outside the university sector, and not enjoying the status of major establishments of higher education, the colleges were among the most local, vocational and distributed parts of English higher education. At a time when less than 13 per cent of school-leavers were 'admitted' into full-time undergraduate education, the pockets of advanced further education provided by the colleges were a relatively open, yet largely hidden and narrowly defined part of a system that, save for the Open University, was otherwise 'elite' in its scale and selectivity.

The local authority presence in higher education, especially within the national planning body created for the non-university sector in 1982, ensured that issues of local access and progression were not ignored. Notwithstanding the local authority concern for the 'seamless robe' of further education, the colleges of further education were to feel the impact of the rise of the polytechnics as national institutions and their desire for greater freedom in running their own affairs. With a 'cap' imposed on the advanced further education pool by the first Thatcher government, the new planning body was under pressure to make savings through a further concentration of advanced work. Inevitably, isolated advanced courses in predominantly non-advanced further education colleges came under particular pressure, although whole higher education institutions were also threatened with closure or amalgamation.

Up to this point, the colleges were part of a single system that had, at one end, courses for young people leaving school with few or no formal qualifications and, at the other, programmes leading to higher degrees. This pattern was broken by the 1988 Act which removed the polytechnics and higher education colleges from the local authorities and established them as free-standing institutions in their own sector and, like the universities, with their own funding council. The colleges whose main concern was non-advanced further education remained, for the time being, with local government. Not only was the local authority interest in higher education now regarded as 'residual'; the higher education work of the remaining local authority colleges was administered and funded in two separate ways. All full-time higher diplomas and any first degree and postgraduate programmes were henceforth the responsibility of the new funding council for the polytechnics and higher education colleges. Other courses, including all part-time higher certificates, continued to be funded through the local authorities. In administration regulations, this separation was inscribed in a distinction between 'prescribed' and 'non-prescribed' higher education respectively.

In this way, English higher education was divided between three sectors – the universities, the polytechnics and higher education colleges, and local authority further education – with colleges in the local authority sector formally relegated, in policy terms at least, to a minor and marginal role in respect of their higher education. Five years later, the 1992 legislation abolished the binary divide, unified the two higher education sectors, and created a new further education sector for the colleges. Like their polytechnic predecessors, the further education colleges were removed from local government and given their own funding body. Between the 1988 and 1992 Acts, and for another two years, higher education in England experienced a dramatic phase of expansion that moved the system from an elite to a mass scale of activity. These two pieces of legislation placed colleges outside the mainstream of higher education, yet their contribution to this growth was neither passive nor inconsequential.

Growth trajectories: the English way

Although much reduced by the 1988 Act, the overall size of the local authority part of higher education was considerable. At least 92 colleges had prescribed courses and about 300 were funded for their non-prescribed programmes. Over 100,000 students were enrolled on these courses, most studying part-time and the great majority pursuing sub-degree qualifications. A contemporary survey report from Her Majesty's Inspectorate described this provision as 'substantial and diverse'. Apart from its accessibility in terms of location, duration, mode and lower entry requirements, the higher education found in the colleges included courses that met a specific demand (usually local but occasionally national), some in unusual subject areas, and those for which there was high demand. In increasing the variety and geographical spread of higher education in England, the colleges played an important part in 'widening opportunities for students' (Department for Education and Science, 1989).

Without a central funding or planning body to promote and nurture their higher education, and without the reputational profile and critical mass of the major providers, the features that made colleges locally accessible were no match for the pull on student demand exercised by the newly incorporated polytechnics and the established universities. Over the peak years of expansion, between 1989 and 1994, overall numbers in English higher education grew by nearly 60 per cent and the participation rate for young people in full-time undergraduate education nearly doubled, from 16 per cent to around 30 per cent. Over the same period, the number of higher education students in further education colleges increased by about one-fifth and this growth was among the slowest recorded across all parts of the higher education system (Table 4.1).

After more than a decade of negligible improvement in the proportion of the age grade enrolled in English undergraduate education, the breakthrough to mass levels of participation was achieved at a speed and under conditions that surprised most commentators. In a reversal of previous policy, a new education minister in the second Thatcher government announced a 'revised' policy on access and a modest expansion in numbers based on increased and widened participation for both young and mature entrants. In the White Paper of 1987 that heralded this change and the associated reforms contained in the 1988 Act, the government planned for steady growth up to 1990 and, following a sharp demographic

Table 4.1: Full-time and part-time students in higher education by type of institution and level or course, England, 1989/90–1994/95 (thousands)

	1989/90	1994/95	(% change)
Higher education institutions (including Open University)			
Postgraduate			
Full-time	61.5	106.1	
Part-time	61.8	147.5	
All	123.3	253.6	(+106%)
First degree			
Full-time	399.3	669.8	
Part-time	99.8	152.2	
All	499.1	822.0	(+65%)
Other undergraduate			
Full-time	61.0	94.6	
Part-time	103.2	107.0	
All	164.2	201.6	(+23%)
Total in higher education institutions	**786.6**	**1277.2**	**(+63%)**

	1989/90	1994/95	(% change)
Further education colleges			
Postgraduate			
Full-time	0.2	0.3	
Part-time	1.7	1.9	
All	1.9	2.2	(+16%)
First degree			
Full-time	3.4	9.6	
Part-time	2.0	3.0	
All	5.4	2.6	(+133%)
Other undergraduate			
Full-time	18.1	33.1	
Part-time	85.8	83.7	
All	103.9	116.8	(+12%)
Total in further education colleges	**111.2**	**131.6**	**(+18%)**
Total all institutions	**897.8**	**1408.8**	**(+57%)**

Notes: 1. Figures for franchise students were not collected for these years and are therefore not indicated.
(Sources: Department for Education/Department for Education and Employment and Ofsted Departmental Reports.)

decline in the size of the school-leaver population, a return to current intake levels in the mid-1990s (Department of Education and Science, 1987). In the event, a combination of buoyant demand and student places funded at a lower unit of resource saw official participation projections reached ahead of time and then surpassed.

The bulk of this great expansion was taken by the higher education establishments and led by the polytechnics. Furthermore, most of this increase was at the first degree and postgraduate levels, and most was for full-time rather than part-time participation. In other words, the English moved to mass higher education by absorbing greater numbers into its core institutions, its regular degrees and its full-time undergraduate courses for which, since the 1960s, the State had borne the costs of tuition and a student maintenance grant.

In requiring the creation of no new or alternative institutions, and no reform of the standard entry and exit qualifications of higher education, the enlarged system retained its broad shape. This was slightly less true for the distribution of students than for the number and type of institutions. As a result of their faster rate of growth, the polytechnics and higher education colleges increased their share of numbers to just over half the total student population. Their success in achieving the 'efficient expansion' demanded by ministers, and executed through the market-like policies of the new funding councils, was rewarded by the Major government with the extension of degree-awarding powers and university titles to each of the polytechnics and a number of the major higher education colleges. The 1992 Act that introduced these changes also established a single funding structure and a common quality assurance framework for a unitary sector of higher education.

Impressed by the way that the polytechnics had 'made the most' of their independence from local government, the same legislation was used to transfer the further education colleges, along with sixth form colleges, to a new sector of further education. The 100 or so sixth form colleges that joined the new sector were previously under school regulations where they offered academic courses, especially A-levels, to full-time students aged 16 to 19. Their inclusion in the new further education sector meant that there were now more students in this age group studying for A-levels than in secondary school sixth forms. In the following years, many sixth form colleges broadened their intakes and introduced vocational and pre-vocational courses to cater for the 'less academically inclined'.

One other consequence of the 1992 Act was that the funding council for further education inherited formal responsibility for non-prescribed higher education and the unitary funding body for higher education assumed responsibility for prescribed higher education. Both funding bodies also had a statutory duty to make provision for assessing the quality of the education they supported. No such duty had been imposed on the binary sectors of higher education, although Her Majesty's Inspectorate had been responsible for monitoring standards in non-university institutions. Now, courses of non-prescribed higher education were assessed by the further education inspectorate and courses of prescribed higher education were assessed through the funding council for higher education.

For higher education in the colleges, then, a similar division of funding responsibilities was followed after 1992 as first introduced in 1988. In the expansionist and more competitive environment for higher education, the college share of higher education enrolments was reduced, from 15 per cent in 1989 to 12 per cent in 1994. However, these figures disguise an indirect or supplementary contribution to higher education made by the colleges over this period and which, 10 years later, was endorsed by the Blair administration as the major vehicle for renewed growth in the first decade of the new century. This was the role of colleges in delivering the teaching of higher education programmes (or parts of programmes) sub-contracted to them under franchise arrangements.

Among the forms of collaboration between higher and further education establishments that developed in the closing years of the local authority system, franchising was a small and isolated development (Abramson, Bird and Stennett, 1996). That was changed by the greater independence given to the polytechnics and their willingness to engage in accelerated growth. Given the pace of later expansion, and its unplanned and under-funded nature, franchising enabled higher education institutions to take up 'capacity at the margin', especially when their own campuses were unable to accommodate more students.

Franchising was pioneered and led by some of the fastest-expanding polytechnics, with one or two institutions operating franchises with as many as 20 colleges. By the time that expansion was brought to a halt in 1994, it was estimated that up to 40,000 students were taught on franchised or collaborative programmes (Parry, 1997). If these are included in the number of students undertaking their higher education in further education, the college proportion of all higher education students was roughly the same as that at the beginning of the growth era.

For their part, the colleges were equally active and attracted by franchise activity, with several entering into agreements with more than one higher education institution. Equipped with delegated financial responsibility by the 1988 Act and set ambitious growth targets following the 1992 Act, the colleges were keen to demonstrate their own growing independence. Not only did franchising bring benefits for students by extending opportunities for access and transfer; it offered further education staff the experience of higher level (and higher status) teaching and it provided the college with a welcome additional source of income. Collaborative arrangements increased the local availability of higher education, taking new courses and new subjects into colleges, enhancing progression within and between partner institutions, and bringing some colleges into higher education for the first time. Apart from their franchise programmes and the courses of higher education they provided in their own right, the other major contribution of colleges to mass participation was the plurality and popularity of their access to higher education pathways. During the 1980s, the colleges of further education were the only institutions that prepared and qualified students through the three main entry routes recognised by the 1987 White Paper: traditional sixth form qualifications (A-levels); vocational qualifications; and 'access courses'. While the school-based A-level route retained its dominance throughout the expansion years, an increasing number of students were using the colleges to take or re-take their upper secondary qualifications and more and more adults were opting for college-based access courses as an alternative route into higher education.

Reform of the specialist A-level examinations had been ignored or rejected by successive governments, but the local authority further education colleges, in association with the polytechnics, had been successful nevertheless in negotiating linked access programmes and broadening admissions arrangements for 'non-traditional' students. Access courses targeted at women, black and working-class students, and leading to 'guaranteed' places on selected undergraduate courses, were probably the closest the English came to positive action in higher education. Collaborative partnerships of this kind only accounted for a small percentage of the new students entering higher education but, in many instances, they paved the way for the growth of franchise relationships between the same institutions (Fulton, 1989).

Franchise developments were just one of the features that distinguished the college contribution to mass expansion in England from its neighbours in Scotland, Wales and Northern Ireland. Only in Wales was franchising a noteworthy activity: not because it was a widespread phenomenon but because, unlike the scattered and unregulated growth in England, its adoption was planned and controlled by the Welsh funding body (Griffiths, 2003). Outside England and Wales, it was higher education offered in their own name that accounted for nearly all the expansion in higher education numbers at further education colleges.

Nowhere was this more evident than in Scotland. Not only did this country have a quarter of its higher education students already enrolled in the colleges at the beginning of the expansion period; these institutions were the fastest to expand within the Scottish system (Table 4.2).

As a result of this pattern of growth, Scotland emerged with two 'parallel' systems of higher education (Gallacher, 2002): a college system responsible for the greater part of sub-degree higher education and a set of higher education establishments engaged mainly in first degree and postgraduate education. The strong presence of higher education in the colleges contributed importantly to the higher participation rates in Scotland, rivalled only by those in Northern Ireland where college-based higher education was proportionally smaller and where, territorially, access was severely constricted by an under-supply

Table 4.2: Higher education students by type of institution and country, United Kingdom 1989/90–1993/94 (thousands)

	1989/90	1993/94	(% change)
England			
Higher education institutions	688.4	1044.2	(+52%)
Further education colleges	119.2	146.4	(+23%)
Proportion in further education			
colleges	15%	12%	
Age participation index	16%	28%	
Scotland			
Higher education institutions	98.5	132.5	(+35%)
Further education colleges	33.1	47.3	(+43%)
Proportion in further education			
colleges	25%	26%	
Age participation index	23%	35%	
Wales			
Higher education institutions	45.6	72.5	(+59%)
Further education colleges	1.6	1.1	(–31%)
Proportion in further education			
colleges	4%	1%	
Age participation index	19%	32%	
Northern Ireland			
Higher education institutions	23.8	32.6	(+37%)
Further education colleges	3.4	5.1	(+50%)
Proportion in further education			
colleges	12%	14%	
Age participation index	24%	33%	

Notes:

1. Figures for franchise students were collected for these years and therefore not indicated.

2. The API for England is the number of English domiciled initial entrants to full-time and sandwich undergraduate higher education aged under 21, expressed as a percentage of the average number of 18- and 19-year-olds in the England population. Similarly for Scotland, Wales and Northern Ireland. *(Sources: Department for Education and Skills, Further Education Statistical Record, Scottish Office, Universities Statistical Record and Welsh Office.)*

of undergraduate places (Cormack, Gallagher and Osborne, 1997). Significantly, the percentage gap in participation levels between Scotland on the one side and England and Wales on the other was little changed over these years, even though overall rates of increase were greater for the English and the Welsh.

The English encounter with mass higher education left the colleges with a displaced, more differentiated and less secure pattern of higher education. Eclipsed by the rise of the polytechnics and other large higher education providers, and with student demand focused overwhelmingly on full-time courses leading to the full-time first degree, the sub-degree programmes offered by colleges in their own name were less attractive to the new wave entrants who, in the English manner, equated the first degree with a 'real' higher education.

Although there had been an upward drift in balance of higher education provided by the polytechnics and some of the higher education colleges, they still retained a fair amount of full-time provision at the sub-degree levels. Since these courses were often run alongside or in association with modular degree programmes, they provided a safety valve for candidates admitted with different, fewer or weaker qualifications. Students initially enrolled for the honours degree might complete their studies with an 'intermediate' or sub-degree qualification. Alternatively, those recruited to sub-degree courses might have the opportunity to transfer to the first degree track (Fulton and Ellwood, 1989).

The access advantage that sub-degree provision brought to the polytechnics was a source of disadvantage to further education colleges unable to provide internal progression to the first degree. On the other hand, the network of franchise and other collaborative relationships that colleges operated in partnership with higher education establishments extended the progression options and pathways available to students studying in college settings. The variety and complexity of the provision that evolved in, through and around the colleges was considerable, yet one consequence of this cross-sector activity was to obscure and confuse the identity of college-based higher education.

For all the higher education effort expended by individual colleges, these institutions were now detached, structurally and culturally, from the central authorities responsible for higher education. Further education institutions might be funded for some of their courses by the new funding council for higher education but, unlike for establishments within the higher education sector, this body had no responsibility for the institutional well-being of college providers. That was the responsibility of the new funding council for further education. Since higher education was neither central nor integral to the mission of the new further education sector, and given that it represented such a small proportion of students in the sector, there was little incentive for the funding council to consider or nurture the higher level work undertaken by the colleges.

When a crisis of funding brought an end to full-time undergraduate expansion in 1994, the colleges were confronted, as before, with a government policy of 'no policy' in respect of the higher education they provided: whether that be prescribed courses funded by the higher education funding body, non-prescribed programmes supported by the further education funding body, or courses franchised to them by higher education establishments.

Renewed expansion: the English experiment

The policy of 'consolidation' imposed on higher education by the Major government prompted bodies like the higher education funding council to consider the current and likely future conditions for undergraduate education. Broadly, there was an expectation that the system would be characterised by a vocational orientation, a demand for new and more flexible patterns of study, a need to widen and support participation across the life span, and a growth of local and regional markets for higher education. Given the congruence between these trends and the 'distinctive features' of higher education in further education, there were strong grounds to suggest that colleges were well placed to respond to future demands. This was particularly the case if policy and funding pressures were to lead to an increasing need for shorter courses, and especially if higher education might be cheaper to provide in the further education sector (Higher Education Funding Council for England, 1995).

At odds with these convergent developments, it was noted, were funding and quality regimes that were increasingly diverse, complex and anomalous. Furthermore, a continuation of the essentially market-led approach to funding was likely to produce 'a disparate and un-coordinated' system. To overcome some of these difficulties, the funding council recommended that the future funding of higher educa-tion in the colleges should be based on 'collaborative' arrangements with higher education establishments. This would probably require a measure of planning, especially at the institutional and local levels. Although not established as a planning body, the higher education funding council might need to be 'more active in steering the approach', especially if undue mission drift was to be avoided (Higher Education Funding Council for England, 1996a).

In the same month that the funding council published its consul-tative report on these matters, the government announced in 1996 the setting-up of a national committee of inquiry into the future of higher education in the United Kingdom under the chairmanship of Sir Ron Dearing (the Dearing Committee, 1996–97). In its written evidence to the Inquiry, the funding council anticipated an increasingly important role for colleges in providing the first cycle of higher education and collaborating with other providers (and employers) to enhance the local and regional dimension:

> As higher education develops in an increasingly modular way, with shorter cycles and more breakpoints between them, further education (FE) colleges might have an increasingly important role to play in providing the first cycle of higher education (HE), particularly in areas relatively remote from HE institutions.

> This suggests further changes in the relationship between further and higher education, an area which is presently very fluid. It also reinforces the need to establish, within a credit framework or otherwise, clear distinctions between levels of study. FE colleges will continue to focus on providing further education and training up to HE level; similarly HE institutions will provide most of what is beyond this level. However, the boundary between the two sectors will not be clear cut, and FE colleges

will continue to develop their role as important providers of HE which is distinct in character and level. To avoid duplication and mission drift, and also to optimise regional coverage, the Higher Education Funding Council for England (HEFCE) believes that there would be merit in requiring the further development of HE in FE to take place in a structured way, based on cooperation between providers of HE in the area concerned. (Higher Education Funding Council for England, 1996b, pp. 19–20)

Having moved to mass higher education, quantitatively at least, without needing to advance or accelerate the college contribution, it was left to a higher education body and not a further education agency to argue the future place of colleges in a more differentiated system of higher education. Moreover, the backdrop for a fundamental review of higher education was a deepening crisis of funding in both sectors and, not without notice, it was only in higher education that an independent committee of inquiry was the chosen instrument to address this problem. In further education, it was an internal committee established by the sector funding body to advise on the strategies to widen participation (the Kennedy Committee, 1994–97) that became the principal instrument for examining and profiling the role of the college sector.

As an illustration of how divided were the dual structures and mentalities of English post-secondary education, the Kennedy and Dearing Inquiries were pursued as quite separate exercises, with no formal exchange of evidence, ideas or personnel between the two (Parry, 2001). More than that, the Kennedy Inquiry was largely innocent of the higher education that belonged to the colleges and its report had nothing to say about the nature or future of this activity (Further Education Funding Council, 1997). The Dearing Committee, by contrast, made specific and major recommendations addressed to the provision of higher education in the further education sector (National Committee of Inquiry into Higher Education, 1997).

In this way, contemporary policy for higher education in the colleges has its origins in the proposals of the Dearing Inquiry, some of which built on the preliminary work of the funding council for higher education. Out of this process, and through the agency of a New

Labour government, higher education in further education was elevated to the status of 'high' policy. The context for this new regard was a resumption of growth in higher education and a policy experiment designed to change the traditional pattern of demand for English undergraduate education. Participation in higher education was intended to approach near universal levels by the year 2010 and, in partnership with universities and employers, the colleges were expected to deliver a substantial amount of this expansion.

Renewed expansion and a special mission

Although overshadowed by the controversy surrounding the introduction of a student contribution to the costs of full-time undergraduate education, the Dearing recommendations on renewed expansion and the college role in higher education also marked a break with previous policies. In looking to a return to significant growth over the next 20 years, the Inquiry expected a major part of future expansion to be expressed at the sub-degree level. To help meet this demand, the committee proposed that, in the medium term, priority in this growth should be accorded to further education colleges and that all such provision should be funded directly by the funding body for higher education. Sub-degree higher education was to become 'a special mission' for the colleges.

To perform this distinctive role and to prevent any upward drift in their higher education, it would be necessary to disallow growth in their first degree and postgraduate work. To reinforce this directly funded mission, responsibility for the funding of all higher education was to pass to the higher education funding body, irrespective of its location. In addition, the use of franchising was to be tightly controlled and regulated. Franchising had expanded rapidly and the Inquiry was concerned that colleges were 'extending themselves too broadly and entering into too many relationships to be able to ensure quality and standards'.

In some of the most prescriptive recommendations in the Dearing Report, 'serial franchising' – where a franchisee transferred public funding to a third party – was to be ruled out and rigorous criteria would be applied to limit 'multiple franchising' such that the franchisee normally had only one higher education partner. Although these prescriptions were subsequently moderated, they signalled a determination to maintain the standards of English undergraduate education under mass conditions, especially if such relationships threatened the national and international standing of the first degree.

In seeking to curb the spread of franchising, concentrate expansion at the sub-degree levels, and fund colleges directly for their leading role in this growth, the Inquiry report provided surprisingly little evidence and analysis to underpin these proposals. Focusing expansion on levels below the first degree would, it was suggested, better reflect the diverse expectations, backgrounds and qualifications of new entrants; support lifelong learning by providing greater flexibility for individuals to enter and exit the system at different points; help reduce dropout and thereby maintain one of the highest first degree graduation rates in the world; and address the relative international disadvantage at the sub-degree and intermediate levels.

Similarly, the case for concentrating future growth on the colleges occasioned little discussion or examination, except for the role of these institutions in making higher education accessible to people in communities for whom geographic or psychological distance was a barrier to participation. Both through their own higher education and their collaboration with establishments in the higher education sector, the further education colleges were seen as 'fundamental to widening participation in higher education'. The affordability argument – that further education might be a cheaper location for higher education – was a muted, if not altogether silent element in the Inquiry report. Nor was the vocational, technical and professional orientation of college-based higher education given the close attention that might have been expected by the 'economic imperative' to resume growth and the need for members of a learning society to 'renew, update and widen their knowledge and skills throughout life'.

However, probably the most important influence guiding this set of recommendations was the scale of participation and the pattern of provision and progression exhibited in Scotland. In the Inquiry report, the higher participation rate in Scotland (44 per cent) compared with

England (33 per cent) was attributed, in part, to a recently introduced structure of qualifications which supported progression from school, through further education and into higher education, and to 'the wide scope there to study sub-degree higher education in further education colleges'. In Scotland, it was reported, about 40 per cent of higher education was at sub-degree levels and over a quarter (27 per cent) of the total provision was delivered by further education colleges. Advised and assisted by a Scottish committee, the Dearing Inquiry was made well aware of the distinctiveness of higher education in Scotland and, most likely, was influential in decision making regarding a number of key matters relating to policy and practice in England.

On one important matter the English chose not to borrow from Scotland: whereas in that country all sub-degree provision in the colleges would be funded by the Scottish further education funding body and the rest of their higher education supported by the Scottish higher education funding body, in England all such provision would be supported by the higher education funding council. The latter option was favoured for England because it was 'closest to the current English model' and since:

> only this could force a consideration of the relative costs of similar provision across all the providing institutions, be they in the further or higher education sector; that this would place enhanced responsibility for funding sub-degree provision squarely alongside that for other higher education; that it would not confuse delivery of sub-degree higher education with the remaining legal duty for further education of the Further Education Funding Councils; that it would be essentially a tidying-up of the current arrangements; and that the development of the sort of sub-degree qualifications with value . . . could only be achieved within the higher education context. (Ibid., p. 355)

In confirming these arrangements, the Dearing Committee ruled against any merging of the funding responsibilities of the two sector councils in England. While there was scope for more cooperation between the two councils, the scale of English higher and further education, the number of institutions, and the need for a funding body 'to relate effectively to them', dictated that this division be continued. Nevertheless, there should be 'stronger arrangements for liaison at regional level, particularly to assist in widening participation'.

What was interesting about these conclusions, and about the proposal to develop higher education in the colleges, was the need for the Dearing Inquiry to range more widely than originally intended. At the outset, the committee chose to resist any broadening of the scope of its studies to embrace 'tertiary' education: 'We had to set some boundaries' and 'We already faced an enormous task.' However, by adopting a conventional definition of higher education and rejecting a tertiary approach, the Inquiry found itself in some difficulty when looking to underpin some of its key recommendations, especially those directed at other sectors, with the foundation of evidence and depth of analysis merited by their strategic importance.

Whatever the warrant, this cluster of proposals and their broad acceptance by the newly elected Blair government, represented the first stage in what was to become a bold policy experiment to modify and diversify the shape of English higher education, not just its funding. For Dearing, this quest rested on an assumption that future demand would favour short cycle qualifications, with more stopping-off points with 'real value' at levels below the first degree, with clearer but flexible pathways 'including academic and vocational components', and with more opportunities for students to return to higher education in later life. As in the years prior to consolidation, the committee saw future participation being determined primarily by student demand, but with employer requirements accorded a central importance and with the State intervening if necessary 'to ensure that levels of participation match those of our competitor nations'.

Stalled demand and a new qualification

From the beginning, the recommendations in support of a special mission for the colleges fell victim to weak demand for sub-degree higher education and some early subject assessment reports that expressed concern about the quality and standards of higher education courses in a small number of colleges. Preoccupied with their own funding problems, it was also apparent that the colleges themselves did not engage collectively or forcefully with the Dearing proposals. Meanwhile, the response within the higher education sector reflected a mixture of indifference, unease and hostility.

In its own response to the Dearing Report, the higher education funding council welcomed the return to growth but was not convinced by the evidence of demand for sub-degree level entry in England or by the argument for any immediate focus on sub-degree provision. The same body was equally uneasy about limiting the expansion of sub-degree courses to the colleges since this might damage or restrict opportunities for similar activity in higher education institutions. Furthermore, how colleges were funded for their higher education was 'more complex' than the Inquiry report assumed (Higher Education Funding Council for England, 1997).

Rather than follow the Dearing precept on direct funding, the funding council offered colleges a choice between three funding options: direct funding; indirect funding (franchising); and funding through a consortium of further and higher education establishments. The justification for plural funding routes and for a strong steer in favour of collaborative arrangements was explained in terms of options 'which best support quality and standards'. The funding body believed it was harder to safeguard quality where there was a small volume of higher education in a college whose focus and mission was oriented towards further education. There was a danger that such provision might become 'isolated' because it was neither securely rooted in the core further education work of the college nor linked through partnerships to the wider higher education community. Central to the funding approach was a concern for the quality and comparability of the student experience:

> Our primary concern is to ensure a high quality of HE experience for the students on all the programmes we fund, irrespective of provider and location. Colleges will be able to choose the funding option which best suits their circumstances. But in making their choices, we look to colleges to consider carefully whether some form of collaboration or partnership with an HEI [higher education institution] or other FECs [further education

colleges] would help them secure high quality and standards. We also expect franchising relationships will continue unless there is good reason to change them. (Higher Education Funding Council for England, 1999, p. 1)

Colleges were able, if they wanted, to continue with multiple funding routes, such as being indirectly funded via a higher education establishment, while being directly funded for other programmes. Nevertheless, the funding council believed that, to avoid unnecessary complexity, it would 'normally make sense' for a college to choose a single funding route for all its higher education provision.

By the time that the new funding approach was introduced in 2000, the higher education funding body had assumed responsibility for all the higher education previously supported by the further education funding council, except for courses leading to higher level professional and vocational qualifications. As a result of this change, together with some colleges choosing to be funded indirectly or through consortia, the total number of colleges receiving funds directly from the higher education funding body rose to over 200 compared to just 70 or so colleges before the transfer of funding responsibility. In contrast to the large number also operating franchise arrangements, only a handful of colleges opted for consortia funding.

In the same way that the transfer of funding after 1999 brought the higher education funding council into direct relationships with many more further education institutions, so the quality assurance agency for higher education had to plan for a greater volume of subject review visits to colleges, many of which had little or no previous experience of the requirements and processes of this organisation. Even before this point, a 'disproportionate' number of college providers of higher education found themselves at the wrong end of summary judgements by the quality assurance agency. At a time when the government looked to the further education sector to provide for growth in higher education, the low ratings achieved by some colleges were viewed as a particular concern and led the agency to question the capacity of these colleges to deliver higher education programmes (Quality Assurance Agency for Higher Education, 2000).

With little evidence of improved demand in the post-Dearing years, ministers came to doubt the fitness and attractiveness of existing sub-degree qualifications to deliver further significant expansion. In order to stimulate demand and serve as the engine for future expansion, the Blair government announced the introduction of a new two-year qualification, described initially as an associate degree but finally (and somewhat confusingly) designated a 'foundation degree'. In parallel with this venture, and equally controversial, the government committed itself to a participation target of 50 per cent of 18- to 30-year-olds entering higher education by the year 2010.

The radical nature of these two interventions was a measure of the seriousness of a policy project aimed at widening access, increasing participation, maintaining standards and, now, transforming vocational higher education. Consistent with the Dearing proposal to locate much of the future expansion of sub-degree higher education in the colleges, these twin measures marked the second and fullest expression of the policy push to concentrate growth in the first and early cycles of undergraduate education.

The 50 per cent target had its origin in the New Labour manifesto for the 2001 general election and was subsequently adopted with no explanation for the level and timing of the target or for the new definition it brought into being. With political devolution implemented in Scotland, Wales and Northern Ireland after 1999, the target was developed essentially for England. At the time of the election, Scotland was already on the point of recording 50 per cent of young people undertaking some form of higher education by the time they were aged 21, whereas in England around one in three young people were entering full-time undergraduate education. Whatever the rationale for a figure of 50 per cent, the target placed more urgency and energy behind the policy of renewed growth. It also required a steeper curve of expansion than the 45 per cent participation rate for young people thought achievable by the Dearing Committee over the next 20 years.

In large part, the foundation degree was created to build demand for a different kind of higher education and, in so doing, achieve most of the expansion required to meet this target. By involving employers in its design and operation, and by enabling students to apply their learning to specific workplace situations, the foundation degree was intended to raise the value of work-focused higher education and, over time, subsume many of the other qualifications at these levels, including the higher national diplomas and certificates whose numbers had 'begun to fall away'. Although of value in its own right, the new qualification was also expected to lay the basis for widening participation and progression to an honours degree (Higher Education Funding Council for England, 2000a; Department for Education and Employment, 2000b).

To promote its accessibility, the new degree was to be delivered 'typically' by further education colleges. To ensure its credibility, on the other hand, the development of foundation degrees was expected to be conducted in 'consortia' led by an institution with degree-awarding powers, usually a university, that would not only validate and vouchsafe the qualification but 'guarantee' arrangements for progression to the first degree. In rejecting a national validation system for the new qualification and requiring colleges to become partners (with employers) in consortia, the government demonstrated an unwillingness to trust further education with ownership and leadership of the new award. Where once franchise-type relationships were officially viewed with caution, they were now seen as the normal and preferred means by which colleges might augment their higher education provision. In the event, 21 consortia were approved to deliver the new qualification from 2001, each in receipt of development funding to launch the first prototype courses.

The foundation degree was the first major new higher education qualification to be introduced into the English system since the diploma of higher education in the 1970s. The issue of credibility, so important to the Blair administration, had been one of the main reasons why the Dearing Committee had rejected the introduction of an 'associate degree' along the lines proposed in an earlier government-funded report on credit accumulation and transfer (Higher Education Quality Council, 1994). Both the shortcomings of existing sub-degree qualifications and, more generally, the failure to provide a robust and high-standard ladder of progression in work-based learning were sufficient, however, to overcome previous objections, including the suspicion that such an award would pave the way to a two-year entitlement for undergraduate education.

Sector reform, re-regulation and deregulation

In parallel with the development of the foundation degree, and as part of a larger strategy to bring education and employment into closer relationship, 'a new vocational ladder' was put forward to span the secondary and post-secondary systems (Blunkett, 2001). At the upper end of the ladder was the foundation degree which provided a vocational route into higher education for those qualifying with upper secondary qualifications or through the award of credits for appropriate prior and work-based learning. Employees looking to upgrade their skills were a key target group for the foundation degree, and its wide range of modes of delivery, including part-time, modular, distance and work-based study, was expected to be more aligned to 'earning and learning' than existing provision.

At the other end of the ladder, more vocational versions of second-ary qualifications were to be introduced for 14- to 16-year-olds which would open a pathway to more advanced programmes that were predominantly vocational or which combined academic and vocational study. Having already established itself as the principal location for young people and adults undertaking qualifying programmes leading to higher education, the further education sector was poised to supply qualifications at each of the main levels in the new vocational ladder.

Cutting across these attempts to create cross-sector partnerships and progression pathways was a major reform of the post-secondary sector that reaffirmed the boundary between higher and further education. Following the Learning and Skills Act of 2000, the further education sector was abolished and replaced by a larger post-compulsory sector under a single body – the Learning and Skills Council – which took responsibility for the strategic development, planning, funding and quality assurance of post-16 learning 'excluding higher education' (Department for Education and Employment, 1999).

Described as 'the most significant and far reaching reform ever enacted to post-16 learning in this country', the new council assumed funding responsibility for all further education colleges, for sixth forms in schools (from the local authorities), for government-funded training and workforce development (from the training and enterprise councils), and for adult and community learning (from local government). In the same way, the existing inspection systems responsible for schools, colleges and work-based training were brought together within a single framework.

Now expected to compete and cooperate with other organisations in the new sector, the colleges found their core provision planned and coordinated locally, through a network of 47 local learning and skills councils. Shortly before their transfer, a 'modernisation' of the colleges was announced 'to meet the challenge of the knowledge economy'. Central to this vision was a sharpening of the distinctiveness and specialist focus of colleges: 'The need first and foremost for each college to identify what it is best at, and to make that field of excellence central to its mission' (Department for Education and Employment, 2000a). By 2005, 50 per cent of general further education colleges were planned to have 'an established vocational specialism for which they are regarded as a centre of excellence locally, regionally and nationally'. That target was subsequently brought forward to 2004 and the first sixteen 'pathfinder' colleges were announced in 2001.

The reform strategy for the whole of the learning and skills sector, including its more than six million 'learners' and over 4,000 providers, involved a new system of targets and performance management, strategic area reviews to assess the pattern of provision in each part of the country, and collaborative working between colleges and schools across the 14 to 19 phase of learning. On the links with higher education, described in just four out of 126 paragraphs in the strategy document, the key objectives were two-fold: to encourage young people with level 3 vocational qualifications to progress to higher education (only around 50 per cent did so, compared to around 90 per cent of those with two or more A-level qualifications); and to extend the strong partnerships already in place between schools, colleges, other providers and universities to widen participation and support increased progression. For colleges that delivered higher education, it was important once more:

that any expanded provision is of high quality and is consistent with the
distinct mission locally which we are looking for colleges to develop.
(Department for Education and Skills, 2002, p. 26)

Sector reform and college modernisation were intended to deliver a
more integrated approach to lifelong learning, but for further
education establishments offering higher education the survival of
sector divisions meant a continuing engagement with a dual structure
and a binary apparatus for education beyond the compulsory phase. As
in 1988 and 1992, the 2000 Act reproduced and reinforced a firm
separation between the higher education sector on the one side and the
further education and training system on the other.

In a statement echoing arguments in the Dearing Report, the 1999
White Paper that foreshadowed the Act gave two reasons for not
granting the Learning and Skills Council direct funding
responsibility for higher education. The first involved a claim to the
uniqueness of higher education: its contribution was international
and national as well as regional and local. Although universities
should be responsive to the needs of local employers and business,
both to meet skills requirements and in the application of research,
they also operated on a wider stage and therefore required a
different approach to funding. The second justification was more
operational: to include higher education would undermine one of the
main aims of the reform, which was to bring order to an area that
was overly complex. Broadening its purpose to include higher
education would, it was claimed, complicate this remit significantly.

Like the further education funding body at the beginning of its
tenure, the Learning and Skills Council inherited responsibility for
those courses leading to higher level vocational qualifications. The
funding body for higher education continued to support all
undergraduate and postgraduate education, including that in the
colleges. Unlike the institutions of higher education which had
persuaded the government to grant them a 'lighter touch' method of
external quality assessment, the colleges were required to submit to
continuation of a comprehensive programme of full-scale subject
reviews of their directly funded provision. For their franchised courses,

the colleges would come under the new audit processes applied to their partner higher education institutions. In the same document that reported criticism by the colleges of these separate arrangements, the quality assurance agency for higher education used the results of the latest cycle of subject reviews to repeat its concerns about the quality and standards of higher education in a minority of further education colleges (Quality Assurance Agency for Higher Education, 2001).

Low-trust relationships with the colleges were evident again when the Blair government unveiled its access and funding plans to increase participation for English students in higher education from its present 43 per cent 'towards' the 50 per cent target set for the end of the decade. The 2003 White Paper on higher education that re-stated this 'relatively modest' ambition wanted the bulk of this expansion to come through new types of qualification that would help close the 'skills gap' at the associate professional and higher technician levels. These were the employment levels expected to experience the greatest growth in the coming years and, as before, it was work-focused qualifications below the first degree that were believed best suited 'to meet the demands of employers and the needs of the economy and students'. However:

> Work-focused courses at these levels have suffered from social and cultural prejudice against vocational education. Employers claim that they want graduates whose skills are better fitted for work; but the labour market premium they pay still favours traditional three-year honours degrees over two-year work-focused ones. And students have therefore continued to apply for three-year honours courses in preference. We must break this cycle of low esteem, to offer attractive choices to students about the types of course they can undertake. (Department for Education and Skills, 2003b, p. 17)

Henceforth, employer-focused foundation degrees were to become the standard two-year higher education qualification in England and, in order to 'catalyse' a change in the pattern of provision', the government proposed to 'incentivise' both the supply and demand for foundation degrees. On the supply side, additional funded places for foundation degrees would be offered in preference to first degree courses, together with development funding for institutions and employers to work together in designing more new foundation degrees. On the demand side, bursaries might be used either for extra maintenance or to offset the fee charged for the course.

The significance of the latter was that the White Paper proposed to deregulate the current fee arrangements and, from 2006, allow higher education providers to set their own tuition fee for individual courses, up to an agreed maximum. Under this scheme, students would no longer be liable for an up-front fee. Instead, they would repay their contribution, through the tax system and above a minimum income threshold, once they were in employment. In addition to the existing student loan entitlement, a new national grant would be introduced for those from lower-income families. How universities and colleges might respond to this 'financial freedom', and how fee levels might be set for in-house and franchised versions of the same programme, were unknown.

The White Paper proposals were the third and latest stage in the post-Dearing experiment to alter the traditional pattern of demand for English higher education. Alongside the deregulation of fees and the removal of research degree awarding powers as a future requirement to become a university, there were other measures which exposed further education colleges to potentially more competition from rival providers and which signalled a re-regulation of funding partnerships by the State.

The special mission that Dearing had in mind for the colleges was a less protected one in the 2003 White Paper, although this goal had been eroded in the intervening years. Further education would continue to play an important role in serving the higher education needs of local students, but it would not occupy a monopoly or independent position in the delivery of foundation degrees. While foundation degrees would 'often' be delivered in further education settings, the intention to concentrate research funding in a smaller number of universities and to hold 'steady' the numbers studying three-year degree courses was likely to increase competition between institutions for the additional funded places available for foundation degrees.

At the same time, opportunities for colleges themselves to bid for these places would be curtailed. Only where 'niche' provision was delivered, or where there were no obvious higher education partners, would colleges be permitted to apply for directly funded places. In future, these would be considered on a case by case basis and 'against criteria which will include critical mass, track record on quality and standards, and nature of provision'. The remainder, if they had not done so already, would need to combine with partner higher education institutions.

> Further education has strengths in providing ladders of progression for students, particularly for those pursuing vocational routes, and serves the needs of part-time students and those who want to study locally. Further education colleges make an important contribution to meeting local and regional skills needs, including through the higher education they provide. We want this significant role to continue and to grow. However, it will be important that any expanded provision is of the high quality that we expect from higher education. We believe that structured partnerships between colleges and universities – franchise or consortium arrangements with colleges funded through partner HEIs – will be the primary vehicles to meet these aims and will deliver the best benefits for learners. (Ibid., p. 62)

In these circumstances, the only opportunity for most colleges to deliver foundation courses was likely to be through 'structured partnerships'. In the case of franchising, colleges were dependent on a higher education partner for the validation, funding and quality assurance of these programmes, with the university or higher education establishment retaining a percentage of the total funding for the services it provided. In the case of consortium arrangements – only a small proportion of funding partnerships at present – more equal relationships were likely to pertain, although here too a proportion of the total funding was retained by the 'lead' institution (Higher Education Funding Council for England, 2003b).

To support colleges in their partnerships and to help widen their choice of validating universities, a new national network was to be established – Foundation Degree Forward – that would also act as a centre for foundation degree expertise and a link with occupational and professional bodies involved in drawing up frameworks for foundation degrees in new areas of the economy. More generally, the government committed itself to remove 'unnecessary bureaucracy' that stood in the way of 'sensible partnerships' between the two sectors. Less than three years after the passage of the Learning and Skills Act, there was an acknowledgement that 'unnecessary difficulties for collaboration' were presented by the need to respond to two funding regimes and to juggle the requirements of two quality assurance and inspection arrangements. Greater integration of the two systems was anticipated, yet no merger of the two funding councils, as agreed in Scotland.

Near universal access: identity and sustainability

Casting a transatlantic eye on British and English higher education during the 1980s, the author of the original elite-mass-universal model was struck by the vast gulf that existed between further and higher education. For Trow, they were 'simply not part of a common system of post-secondary education' and there was 'enormous resistance in the UK to placing further education in the same planning frame with higher education'. In his view, this disconnection was one of several features constraining the diversity of higher education and impeding its future growth (Trow, 1987; 1989). In the years immediately following these judgements, English higher education moved suddenly and swiftly to mass levels of participation and, since 1997, has embarked on another phase of expansion that will take the system close to the kind of conditions that Trow associated with universal access.

In the transition from elite to mass higher education and, now in pursuit of the 50 per cent target, the fiscal, planning and policy division between further and higher education was maintained, even reinforced. Rather than inhibiting cross-border relationships, the passage to mass higher education was characterised by an increasing diversity and density of collaborative arrangements. Nevertheless, the dominance of the full-time first degree in the English system, together with the capacity of existing higher education institutions to attract and absorb greater numbers at lower costs, left the colleges with an ancillary rather than a leading role in the expansion period.

As charted in this paper, one major legacy of this growth was a marked ambivalence and anxiety about locating renewed expansion in further education institutions. When colleges were allowed a more prominent role, this was generally conditional upon funding partnerships that, in the case of franchise arrangements, 'necessarily involved a hierarchical relationship between the franchiser and the franchisee'. In a franchise partnership, it was the higher education institution that was 'fully responsible' for the students, including 'all aspects' of the finance, administration and quality of the student experience (Higher Education Funding Council for England, 2000b).

All the same, following the 2003 White Paper, it was still possible for directly funded further education colleges to apply for additional foundation degree places in their own name, along with details of the quality assurance arrangements of the validating higher education institution, the involvement of the employer in the design and regular review of the programme, and the nature of articulation arrangements allowing progression to at least one honours degree. It was also recognised that higher education establishments might wish to deliver a proportion or perhaps the whole of the foundation degree programme. Here, as in its response to some of the Dearing recommendations directed at the colleges, the funding body for higher education adopted a more nuanced position than that outlined in the White Paper. Not only did the funding council expect colleges to 'play a major role' in the delivery of foundation degrees, but it insisted that, where no college was involved in the partnership, the bid 'should indicate why this was not possible or appropriate' and 'should explain the strategy for delivering the programme' (Higher Education Funding Council for England, 2003a).

Although at the heart of a policy project to change the traditional pattern of demand for undergraduate education, the colleges have experienced conditions less than favourable to the achievement of a clear mission and identity in relation to higher education. At the time they entered the new learning and skills sector, there were roughly

Table 4.3: Students undertaking higher education and higher level qualifications in higher education institutions and further education colleges by level and type of qualification, England, 2000/01 (thousands)

	Students taught at higher education institutions	Students taught at further education colleges	All students
Postgraduate	282.2	8.0	290.2
First degree	761.9	24.9	786.8
Other undergraduates	183.7	91.2	274.9
Higher national diploma	24.4	39.6	63.9
Higher national certificate	5.6	43.1	48.7
Diploma of higher education	47.1	1.7	48.8
Certificate of higher education	15.7	0.6	16.3
Other undergraduate diplomas and certificates	56.8	4.3	61.1
Professional qualifications at undergraduate level	19.7	0.2	19.9
Other qualifications at undergraduate level	14.4	1.8	16.2
Higher level qualifications	–	*63.1*	*63.1*
National vocational qualifications at levels 4 and 5	–	20.8	20.8
Other higher level qualifications	–	42.4	42.4
Institutional credit	*237.5*	*0.1*	*237.6*
All levels and types of qualification	**1465.3**	**187.3**	**1652.6**

Notes:
1. Figures for further education colleges include franchise students.
2. Figures for institutional credit include all Open University students.
(Sources: FEFC; HEFCE.)

187,000 students undertaking higher education and higher level qualifications in further education institutions in England. Distributed across some 340 colleges, these students accounted for one in nine (11 per cent) of the total higher education population or, if postgraduate education was excluded, around one in seven (15 per cent) of those studying for undergraduate and higher level qualifications (Table 4.3).

By 2002, about 12,000 people were studying for foundation degrees and, by 2006, it was hoped to have 50,000 places available for this qualification (Department for Education and Skills, 2003a).

Unlike in Scotland, where most short cycle vocational qualifications belong to further education institutions, the colleges and higher education establishments in England pursue a shared or overlapping mission in respect of sub-degree higher education. The higher national diploma and certificate continue to be offered by both sectors in England and, although more of these two qualifications are taught in the colleges than elsewhere, the higher education institutions are nevertheless the largest providers of undergraduate education at levels below the first degree. Some of this larger share is due to the near monopoly of diploma and certificate of higher education courses in nursing which have no real presence in the colleges.

Put another way, the growth trajectory of English higher education over the last 20 years has not provided the colleges with a discrete or cohesive mission to distinguish their programmes, by title or level, from those in establishments of higher education. Over time, the expansion of the foundation degree is expected to incorporate and reduce the present variety of college-based higher education qualifications and so enable further education to become the normal location for the new standard two-year higher education qualification. Much will depend on future demand for the foundation degree, especially in a deregulated market for undergraduate fees, and the extent to which the qualification is delivered wholly or partly by further education colleges. What is less likely to change, at least in the short term, is the requirement on colleges to look to the validating universities for the quality assurance of the delivery of the foundation degree and, in many cases, for the funding of its teaching as well.

In a situation where fewer than 60 colleges are currently responsible for half the total number of students studying for higher education and higher-level qualifications, the question of the scale, scope and sustainability of this provision is an open question. Several of the colleges with the largest student numbers have argued in favour of concentration of higher education in a limited number or range of further education institutions. Whether expressed in terms of economies of scale, their infrastructures and mature experience of higher education, or the benefits which critical mass can bring to the quality of the student experience, some of these colleges have regarded themselves as quite different from other further education establishments; and, because of the size of their higher education, they have sought to be treated differently by the relevant authorities.

If, as intended, structured partnerships between universities and colleges become the primary vehicles to deliver growth of higher education in the colleges, then a dispersed pattern of provision is probably set to continue. Franchising and funding through recognised consortia have already become important and distinctive features of higher education in further education. By 2002, over half the total of higher education establishments and around two-thirds of further education institutions in England were party to such arrangements. The proportion of franchise students taught on courses of prescribed higher education was estimated at 30 per cent and their numbers were particularly strong for full-time first degree and higher diploma courses. While full-time students were a majority on franchised courses, they were a minority on the prescribed programmes which colleges offered in their own right. In short, one of the effects of indirect funding was to introduce yet more diversity and complexity into the college contribution to higher education (Parry, Davies and Williams, 2003).

For all the policy focus on foundation degrees and their delivery by the colleges, these institutions remain further education establishments. The greater part of their activity is concerned with learning at other levels. The nature of their core provision is shaped by the policy and funding priorities of a sector that has no formal responsibility for higher education. At the local level, the balance of their courses and those of other providers is subject to the judgements and outcomes of strategic area review. How colleges manage their higher education contribution in these uncertain and unstable environments will influence a decision about whether to adjust or abandon the dual arrangements that have overseen the contemporary development of English post-secondary and higher education.

Acknowledgements

The data in Table 4.3 were compiled for a research study undertaken for the Learning and Skills Development Agency and first published in Parry, Davies and Williams (2003). This table is reproduced here by permission of the Learning and Skills Development Agency.

References

Abramson, M., Bird, J. and Stennett, A. (eds) (1996) *Further and Higher Education Partnerships. The Future of Collaboration.* Buckingham: Society for Research into Higher Education and Open University Press.

Blunkett, D. (2001) *Education into Employability: The role of the DfEE in the economy.* London: Department for Education and Employment.

Cantor, L. M. and Roberts, I. F. (1986) *Further Education Today: A critical review.* London: Routledge & Kegan Paul.

Cantor, L., Roberts, I. and Pratley, B. (1995) *A Guide to Further Education in England and Wales.* London: Cassell.

Cormack, R., Gallagher, A. and Osborne, R. (1997) 'Higher Education Participation in Northern Ireland', *Higher Education Quarterly*, Vol. 51, No 1, pp. 68–85.

Department of Education and Science (1987) *Higher Education. Meeting the Challenge*, Cm 114. London: Her Majesty's Stationery Office.

Department of Education and Science (1989) *Aspects of Higher Education in Colleges Maintained by Local Education Authorities. A report by HM Inspectors*, 277/89. London: DES.

Department for Education and Employment (1999) *Learning to Succeed. A New Framework for Post-16 Learning*, Cm 4392. London: The Stationery Office.

Department for Education and Employment (2000a) *Colleges for Excellence and Innovation. Statement by the Secretary of State for Education and Employment on the future of further education in England*. London: DfEE.

Department for Education and Employment (2000b) *Foundation Degrees. Consultation Paper*. London: DfEE.

Department for Education and Skills (2002) *Success for All. Reforming Further Education and Training*. London: DfES.

Department for Education and Skills (2003a) *Foundation Degrees. Meeting the Need for Higher Level Skills*. London: DfES.

Department for Education and Skills (2003b) *The Future of Higher Education*, Cm 5735. London: The Stationery Office.

Fulton, O. (ed.) (1989) *Access and Institutional Change*. Milton Keynes: Society for Research into Higher Education and Open University Press.

Fulton, O. and Ellwood, S. (1989) *Admissions to Higher Education: Policy and practice*. Sheffield: Training Agency.

Further Education Funding Council (1997) *Learning Works. Widening Participation in Further Education*. Coventry: FEFC.

Gallacher, J. (2002) 'Parallel Lines? Higher Education in Scotland's Colleges and Higher Education Institutions', *Scottish Affairs*, Vol. 40, pp. 123–39.

Griffiths, M. (2003) 'Policy-Practice Proximity: The Scope for College-Based Higher Education and Cross-Sector Collaboration in Wales', *Higher Education Quarterly*, Vol. 57, No 4, pp. 355–75.

Higher Education Funding Council for England (1995) *Higher Education in Further Education Colleges: Funding the relationship*. Bristol: HEFCE.

Higher Education Funding Council for England (1996a) *Higher Education in Further Education Colleges: A future funding approach.* Bristol: HEFCE.

Higher Education Funding Council for England (1996b) *Submission by the Higher Education Funding Council for England to the National Committee of Inquiry into Higher Education.* Bristol: HEFCE.

Higher Education Funding Council for England (1997) *Response to the Dearing Report.* Bristol: HEFCE.

Higher Education Funding Council for England (1999) *Higher Education in Further Education Colleges. Guidance for Colleges on Funding Options*, Report 99/24. Bristol: HEFCE.

Higher Education Funding Council for England (2000a) *Foundation Degree Prospectus*, Report 00/27. Bristol: HEFCE.

Higher Education Funding Council for England (2000b) *Higher Education in Further Education Colleges: Codes of practice for franchise and consortia arrangements*, Report 00/54. Bristol: HEFCE.

Higher Education Funding Council for England (2003a) *Foundation Degrees*, Report 2003/48. Bristol: HEFCE.

Higher Education Funding Council for England (2003b) *Review of Indirect Funding Agreements and Arrangements Between Higher Education Institutions and Further Education Colleges.* Bristol: HEFCE.

Higher Education Quality Council (1994) *Choosing to Change. Extending Access, Choice and Mobility in Higher Education.* London: HEQC.

Hyland, T. and Merrill, B. (2003) *The Changing Face of Further Education.* London: Routledge Falmer.

Locke, M., Pratt, J. and Burgess, T. (1985) *The Colleges of Higher Education 1972 to 1982: the central management of organic change.* Croydon: Critical Press.

Matterson, A. (1981) *Polytechnics and Colleges. Control and Administration in the Public Sector of Higher Education*. Harlow: Longman.

National Committee of Inquiry into Higher Education (1997) *Higher Education in the Learning Society. Main Report*. London: NCIHE.

Parry, G. (1997) 'Patterns of Participation in Higher Education in England: A Statistical Summary and Commentary', *Higher Education Quarterly*, Vol. 51, No 1, pp. 6–28.

Parry, G. (2001) *Academic snakes and vocational ladders*. Fourth Philip Jones Memorial Lecture. Leicester: National Institute for Adult Continuing Education.

Parry, G. (2003) 'Mass Higher Education and the English: Wherein the Colleges?', *Higher Education Quarterly*, Vol. 57, No 4, pp. 308–37.

Parry, G. and Thompson, A. (2002) *Closer by Degrees: The past, present and future of higher education in further education colleges*. London: Learning and Skills Development Agency.

Parry, G., Davies, P. and Williams, J. (2003) *Dimensions of Difference: Higher education in the learning and skills sector*. London: Learning and Skills Development Agency.

Pratt, J. (1997) *The Polytechnic Experiment 1965–1992*. Buckingham: Society for Research into Higher Education and Open University Press.

Quality Assurance Agency for Higher Education (2000) *Annual Report and Financial Summary 1998–99*. Gloucester: QAA.

Quality Assurance Agency for Higher Education (2001) *Higher Quality*, 8. Gloucester: QAA.

Scott, P. (1995) *The Meanings of Mass Higher Education*. Buckingham: Society for Research into Higher Education and Open University Press.

Smithers, A. and Robinson, P. (2000) *Further Education Re-formed*. London: Falmer Press.

Trow, M. (1974) Problems in the Transition from Elite to Mass Higher

Education. In *Policies for Higher Education, Organisation for Economic Co-operation and Development*. Paris: OECD.

Trow, M. (1987) 'Academic Standards and Mass Higher Education', *Higher Education Quarterly*, Vol. 41, No 3, pp. 268–92.

Trow, M. (1989) 'The Robbins Trap: British Attitudes and the Limits of Expansion', *Higher Education Quarterly*, Vol. 43, No. 1, pp. 55–75.

Chapter 5

Widening access and diversity of provision: the expansion of short cycle higher education in non-university settings

John Field

The blurring boundaries of higher education

In many countries, the expansion of higher education systems has been accompanied by two closely related developments: the involvement of new types of institution in the provision of higher education and the recognition of shorter periods of study than for the conventional degree. Disparate examples of the first trend include the rapid expansion of private sector higher education institutions (HEIs) in Germany and the Netherlands; the granting of degree-awarding powers in Ireland to the Institutes of Technology (originally created in the 1960s as Regional Technical Colleges); the spread of the corporate university movement; and the more uneven trends in online higher education. This tendency probably reflects a number of factors, the most obvious of which are the prospects of reducing the financial consequences of growth, and tackling what is widely perceived as the extreme conservatism of the university sector.

Examples of the second trend include the adoption within the USA and beyond of two-year Associate Degrees, as well as the more recent embrace of Foundation Degrees in England. A more radical example might be the use of accredited short courses as part of a systematic programme of continuing professional development. Unsurprisingly, short cycle HE has been more widely embraced by non-university actors than by the universities, and this obviously raises the question of how far short cycle qualifications are valued by employers and recognised across the HE system. Perhaps the most elaborate and furthest advanced in the UK is the Scottish Credit and Qualifications Framework, but similar systems exist in Wales and Northern Ireland, with a transnational precedent in the form of the European Credit Transfer System. So as well as developing short cycle higher education, and funnelling some expansion into non-university settings, policy makers have also created credit frameworks that are intended to promote progression.

This pattern has developed across much of the globe since the 1970s, forming part of a wider set of shifts that are now often discussed by policy makers and others through the language of lifelong learning. These trends are part of a wider blurring and erosion of well-established borders between institutions (Edwards, 1997). They can in turn be seen as a response to several different factors, including the capacity of new communications technologies to deliver securely large amounts of information combined with possibilities of remote interaction; the exploding social demand for higher education (the evidence of economic demand is less persuasive); and the perceived rigidities and conservatism of the university sector, which has so far tended very effectively to resist policies designed to secure modernisation and reform. There are also undoubtedly questions of relative cost at stake.

One major justification for the new institutional landscape has been the possibilities that it creates not only of growth, but of widening participation. In England, for instance, the higher education funding body and the Department of Education are agreed on the importance of attracting new types of student into new types of courses within both the universities and the further education (FE) sector. Historically, the

British FE sector was created to provide technical training for young people as part of the transition from school to work, and this remained their core activity until the 1970s. Since the mid-70s, however, the FE sector has diversified considerably, partly in response to government policies designed to introduce a marked degree of marketisation into the sector (Hyland and Merrill, 2003). One market segment into which FE colleges entered with growing confidence from the early 1990s onwards was the provision of higher education. This was far from being either illogical or new: the FE sector had long provided higher level technical training (defined formally as 'advanced further education'), and its entry into the broader HE field was initially slow and incremental; it was also largely unplanned (Gallacher, 2002; Parry, 2003).

Since the mid-1990s, HE within FE has been more systematically embraced by policy makers in Britain. The Dearing and Garrick reports both noted that the FE sector had started to grow its HE provision, and their recommendations encouraged further growth within the FE sector. Their case for doing so rested in part on the grounds that the historical mission and ethos of the FE sector combined with the physical distribution of FE colleges together allowed for a far more inclusive student population than does the university sector (Morgan-Klein, 2003; Parry, 2003).

Since the early 1990s, the scale of HE within FE has expanded considerably, particularly in Scotland. This growth allows us to test the validity of the claims made by policy makers and others over the relationship between equity and expansion. In particular, it allows us to consider the role played by expansion in non-university institutions. One touchstone for the present paper is an unjustly neglected book – neglected at least on this side of the Atlantic – which asked similar questions of the community colleges and historically black universities (HBU) in the USA. In *Elusive Equality*, Lorenzo Morris analysed patterns of participation by African-Americans, and found that they were studying disproportionately in the community college and HBU sectors (Morris, 1979). Morris demonstrated that the expansion of opportunities within the community college and HBU sectors effectively created a segregated track for African-

Americans, which led them into an extremely limited and narrow set of opportunities. African-Americans were far more likely to attend a two-year college than white Americans; those African-Americans who subsequently transferred to a Bachelor's programme after completing their two-year associate degree were more likely to enter a low-status institution than an elite school (Morris, 1979). More recent research into Latino and other minorities has confirmed the tendency of the American system to 'ghettoise' those first-generation college students who opt for the comfort zone of two-year colleges (Goodwin, 2002, p. 19).

The Scottish case allows us to see whether the same pattern is starting to appear in a UK context. Logically, it seems likely that it will. If boundaries are becoming more fluid and open, as Peter Scott points out, the type of mass higher education that has been achieved in the UK and many other Western societies is still rooted in institutions, and borders of some kind or other therefore still exist (Scott, 2000, p. 29). As recent debates over asylum and migration throughout Europe suggest, the possibility of movement across borders can provoke strong defensive reactions, and bring new 'gatekeepers' into the field. It is therefore not at all clear that expanding HE within Further Education Colleges (FECs) will automatically deliver a more accessible and flexible system. And it then follows that expanding HE within FE will not necessarily have the predicted impact upon participation and equity.

HE in FE in Scotland

The scale of higher education within further education colleges in Scotland is striking. In 2001–02, for example, almost one-quarter of all Scottish HE students were said to be studying in FECs (Scottish Executive, 2003b). Many commentators have argued that this pattern of provision is largely responsible for the fact that Scotland has a much higher rate of HE participation than virtually any other European nation. In its strategy for lifelong learning, for example, the Scottish Executive commented that:

> We have much to be proud of, most notably in terms of participation in HE, 28 per cent of which takes place in FE colleges . . . 50 per cent of young people undertake some form of higher education by the time they are 21. The great majority of these courses are vocational in nature. (Scottish Executive, 2003a)

This verdict is also one that is widely shared in the academic community (e.g. Caldwell, 2003). Scotland has long had its own distinctive educational system. In contrast with the rest of the UK, Scottish HE has long had a reputation for accessibility and social openness (Humes and Bryce, 2003). However, the provision of mass HE within the FE sector, alongside the more traditional university institutions, is a relatively recent addition to the educational landscape. Scotland's experience therefore provides an excellent opportunity for examining more broadly the implications of expanding HE provision within an FE context.

HE in FE is largely responsible for the gap between the participation rate in Scotland and that of the rest of Britain. By 2000–2001, just over half of all new entrants to HE were studying in FECs; because their courses are shorter than the three to four years required for a degree, this meant that some 46 per cent of all undergraduate level students in Scotland were in FECs (Morgan-Klein, 2003, p. 340). As Gallacher has shown (2002), this situation resulted from a largely unplanned growth of HE in FECs during the 1980s, which was consolidated during the early 1990s and is now a well-established and relatively stable feature of the Scottish HE scene. Virtually all HE students in Scottish FECs are registered for sub-degree qualifications (Gallacher, 2003, p. 6). Relatively few are taking degrees or other awards; around two-thirds are studying towards Higher Nationals (HNs), accredited through the Scottish Qualifications Agency (SQA). Foundation degrees are virtually unknown in Scotland. As in other parts of the UK, despite growth in full-time numbers over the past decade, much HE provision in FECs remains part-time (Gallacher, 2003, p. 7; Morgan-Klein, 2003, p. 340).

> Scotland therefore presents a marked contrast with the situation in other parts of the UK, both in terms of the sheer scale of HE in FE, and in terms

of the concentration upon HNs. It is not surprising that this is reflected in the Scottish policy framework. The Scottish Executive's review of lifelong learning gave a key role to increased opportunities for articulation and progression between FECs and Higher Education Institutions (HEIs), with substantial additional resources being allocated to promote the use of the Scottish Credit and Qualifications Framework (SCQF). Furthermore, in view of the existing participation rate, the Executive has announced that it 'does not plan any significant further expansion of government-funded places in higher education institutions', but will rather focus on strategies designed to promote retention and articulation across the HE system (Scottish Executive, 2003c, p. 29).

Within an overall context of consolidation around the 50 per cent Age Participation Rate then, the Scottish Executive has made it clear that it sees articulation and progression on the one hand and retention on the other as the two key means of delivering wider participation. It also views Scotland's mass higher education system as critical to economic competitiveness. Yet, while much progression already takes place between FECs and HEIs, its development has been extremely uneven. In the pre-1992 universities, students have progressed on the basis of local arrangements, and they have done so in relatively small numbers. This often meant that the student presented a Higher National Certificate (HNC) as an entry-level qualification, or could claim limited advanced standing for a Higher National Diploma (HND), but this was usually undertaken on an *ad hoc* and often a completely individual and informal basis. In the post-1992 universities, on the other hand, rather larger numbers have progressed from HN programmes in FECs, and they have done so on the basis of formal articulation arrangements. Formal articulation agreements are usually reached on the basis of some curriculum mapping, and lead to 1+3 progression in the case of HNCs and 2+2 in the case of HNDs.

Patterns of institutional differentiation are extremely marked. In the mid-1990s, one survey showed that well over half of all articulation links were with post-1992 universities, and less than one-third with pre-1992 universities; the remainder were with other HEIs (Gallacher, 2002, p. 12). A more recent study confirms this pattern, noting that there is a significant distinction between what the authors call 'recruiting institutions' on the one hand and 'selecting institutions' on the other, with the first group proving keener to explore alternative means of admitting students from FECs than the latter (MacLennan, Musselbrook and Dundas, 2000).

In recent years, the Scottish Executive has identified articulation arrangements as a means of enhancing wider access. In the late 1990s the Scottish Higher Education Funding Council (SHEFC) supported a small number of FE–HE partnerships through its Wider Access Development Grants; subsequently the four SHEFC-funded wider access regional forums were provided with financial support from the Scottish Further Education Funding Council (SFEFC) and their membership was widened to include FECs as well as HEIs. More recently, the Executive has taken some limited steps to widen the range of articulation arrangements so as to foster their use across the HE sector. Rather more significantly, it has also announced detailed plans for merging the two separate funding councils that currently oversee both sectors; this has had the effect of concentrating minds among senior managers in both FECs and HEIs.

Progression in practice

FE–HE transition is relatively well developed within the Scottish system. However, it is also highly differentiated. Arrangements for progression appear to be much more common in some subjects, and in some types of institution, than in others. Systematic studies by Gallacher (2002, 2003) and others have shown that these arrangements also vary considerably in their degree of formality, with some specifying student progression routes in a level of fine detail, while others are fairly informal. The extent to which students can use the SCQF approach (that is, 1+3 or 2+2) rather than negotiate individualised pathways is also highly variable. This section reports on the variety of practice as illustrated both by national data and by two case studies of institutions, conducted as part of a wider project on so-called 2+2 arrangements across the UK.

It is not possible to say with any confidence just how many people progress from an HN on to a degree. While we know that some 6,494 HEI entrants in 2001–02 gave an HNC/D as their highest qualification, there is currently no national information on progression from HE in FE to study in an HEI in Scotland. None the less, the Scottish Executive has made it clear during its review of HE that improved articulation in general, and promotion of 2+2 in particular, will play a central part in the achievement of its goals of wider access and best use of capacity. In particular, the Executive has welcomed the expansion of participation by socially disadvantaged groups in FECs, but expressed disappointment that there had been less movement in the HE sector, and called for action to close 'the access gap' at age 17 (Scottish Executive, 2003c, p. 33).

Recent data suggest that progress towards this goal has been limited. In one national study, McLaurin and Osborne (2002) report that during the late 1990s, some 4,342 students entering Scottish HEIs had listed HNs as their highest entry qualification. Of these, 2,751 – well over half – had entered post-1992 HEIs, and a further 1,064 had entered the Robbins HEIs. Only a twelfth made it into the ancient universities, despite the size of the latter. This study did not look specifically at students who are progressing under formal articulation arrangements – that is, entering with advanced standing on the basis of their earlier higher education studies. Moreover, since these data were collected, the Scottish Credit and Qualifications Framework has been launched, with the aim of providing an underpinning for more systematic progression than was possible under the existing arrangements (http://www.scqf.org.uk/home.aspx). However, more recent data are now available to supplement McLaurin and Osborne's work.

According to the funding council, in 2002–03 some 3,692 student entered HEIs with advanced standing on the basis of a Higher National qualification (SHEFC, 2004). As a share of the total intake, this figure represents under 6 per cent for the year. Out of the total, 67 per cent entered ex-polytechnics and a further eight per cent entered colleges of higher education. At the other end of the spectrum, precisely three students entered the three ancient universities of Glasgow, Edinburgh and St Andrews.

Moreover, there is every sign that articulation arrangements are

Figure 5.1: Estimated regionalisation rate

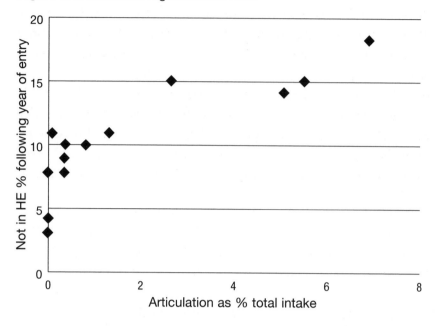

(Source: SHEFC, 2004; HEFCE, 2003.)

strongest where student success rates are weakest. Figure 5.1[1] confirms this pattern for the early years of the current decade, by which time both the experience of articulation and the development of policy were becoming relatively well established. Of course, it is not reasonable to conclude from this that articulation students are more likely to withdraw early from their courses than those who enter under other procedures. What does appear to be the case is that such students generally are eagerly accepted at institutions with higher rates of attrition, and are not generally accepted at institutions with lower rates of attrition. In short, the pattern of progression from HN to degree follows precisely the segregated pathways that Morris discerned in the USA.

Lessons of the Scottish experience

Scotland already leads the UK in 2+2 and similar arrangements (Scottish Executive, 2003c, p. 4)

For many people, Scotland's distinctive pattern of HE participation offers an attractive model, at least at first sight. FECs have shown that they are able to recruit a different type of student from HEIs, with significantly greater proportions coming from disadvantaged backgrounds (Gallacher, 2003; Morgan-Klein, 2003; Scottish Executive, 2003c, p. 33). They have done so for a variety of reasons, none of which appears to be unique to Scotland. For example, FE colleges across the UK are far more likely to be located in or near disadvantaged neighbourhoods than are universities. To some extent then, the Scottish example offers the prospect of direct policy transfer, at least within the UK.

There are also some factors that cannot be found so readily outside Scotland. One distinctive feature is Scotland's size: small enough to allow for effective networks, but large enough to allow for diversity. The academic regulatory framework is also distinctive. FECs have developed large- scale HE programmes in Scotland at least in part because of the role of the SQA. Compared with the institutional complexity and turbulence of the framework surrounding HE in FE in England, the SQA has offered a relatively stable regulatory environment that has allowed FECs to expand their HE provision at a relatively low cost to themselves. At the same time, the regulatory framework has tended to promote the growth of HN provision at the cost of degree programmes in FECs. This has meant that many in HEIs have only a hazy knowledge of what HE is currently provided in FECs, and do not always see the potential for partnership that it represents. Nevertheless, the focus on HNs has also been a considerable asset, since the recognition of HNs by employers and parents has helped to reinforce the regard with which they are held in Scotland, and is consistent with a wider emphasis on forms of higher education that promote employability.

HNs enjoy a positive reputation among employers in Scotland, and this is reflected in the salaries paid to their holders. While the average salary differential in Scotland associated with possession of an HNC/D is roughly half of that associated with possession of a degree, it is still considerably higher than that for other FE qualifications (Gasteen and Houston, 2003). Whereas HNC/D holders in England have been found to earn rates equivalent to those of A-level holders, in Scotland an HN appears to cancel out poor school-leaving qualifications (Gasteen and Houston, 2003).

However, as well as the undoubted benefits to Scotland of the current pattern, there may also be some hidden costs to the growth of HE in FE. The first and most obvious is that in common with the rest of the UK, government in Scotland has failed to tackle the inherited weaknesses of its vocational pathways for young people. Although young Scots are much more likely to stay in education at age 16 than their counterparts elsewhere in the UK, the difference is made up by staying-on rates in school up to the age of 17, and thereafter by participation in HE. FE, and above all skills-intensive employment, are comparatively weak. Indeed, it is possible that the wage differentials studied by Gasteen and Houston (2003) arise at least in part precisely because there is no strong system for developing skilled and intermediate labour. If this is the case, then HNs are substituting for a strong vocational pathway.

Secondly, the headline participation rates in Scottish higher education conceal poor completion rates, particularly in respect of HNs. Completion rates in Scottish further education colleges are not currently published. Figures published on the Funding Councils' website at the time when this paper was in its early stages (but unavailable at the time of publication) suggest that of 12,958 HND candidates in 1999–2000 some 59 per cent were awarded the qualification; 63 per cent of the 18,134 HNC candidates achieved an award (SFEFC, 2000). Similar data from SQA show a considerable gap between candidates entering for an award and those gaining the qualification: in 2002, 75 per cent of candidates entering in a FEC gained an HNC and 64 per cent of those entering for an HND gained the award (SQA, 2003, pp. 144, 148–9). Completion rates for HE in FE are not high, judging by the proportion of candidates who enter for an award successfully.

Moreover, it seems that many students do not reach the stage of entering for an award. In 2001–02, for example, the Funding Council reported that 17,693 students in FECs were working for an HND and 25,429 were studying towards an HNC (figures from www.sfefc.ac.uk/infact, accessed on 30 January 2004). Yet in 2002 the SQA reported only 20,285 entries for HNCs from FECs, and 11,857 for HNDs (SQA, 2003). It seems, therefore, that roughly one-fifth of students on HNC programmes and one-third of those on HND programmes do not get to the stage where they enter with SQA for the award. Behind the headline participation rate, then, it is possible to discern a rather unsatisfactory state of affairs, with significant rates of non-completion and withdrawal.

Nor is this the end of the story. Some HE in FE is very limited in nature indeed, consisting of single HN units taken by young people as a part of another programme. In 2002, for instance, over 12,700 HN candidates had only entered for a single unit, and a further 18,945 were taking between two and five HN units (SQA, 2003, p. 143). So far as the APR is concerned, it might be thought reasonable to ask in what sense individuals in this category may be regarded as 'students entering higher education'. The greater issue, though, surely concerns the rate of withdrawal, non-completion and failure among those who enter HN programmes in FECs. The current levels of achievement pose significant doubts over the efficiency and equity of at least some HE in FE, and must lead us to ask what should be done before this model can be adopted outside Scotland.

Scotland's emerging binary divide

Selective, even discriminatory tracking of this nature is common within higher education systems. Effectively, in the American context, such institutional patterns then tend to confirm and even legitimise ethnic and social class inequalities as students compete in the graduate labour market. A broadly similar pattern is visible in England, where ethnic minority students are more likely to participate in higher education than are white students, but they are much less likely to be studying in pre-1992 universities than they are in the ex-polytechnics, and particularly in the London post-92 institutions (Connor, Tyers, Modood and Hillage, 2004). Scotland's emerging binary divide, then, is by no means unique. Nevertheless, the pattern described here suggests that the constraints on access and equality are powerful ones. The findings are therefore of considerable significance for the policy of expanding higher education through short cycle courses in non-university settings.

The differential distribution of articulation arrangements and short cycle HE has created a multi-track system. Candidates transferring on 1+3 and 2+2 arrangements are most likely to enter the less prestigious institutions. Even within these, they may find themselves further channeled into the least popular subjects, where spare spaces are available for direct entry into the third or second years. There are, therefore, good grounds for supposing that the contribution of 1+3 and 2+2 progression to wider access, while real enough, is nevertheless highly constrained by the differential distribution of existing arrangements. It is also weakened by high rates of withdrawal, non-completion and failure within the FE sector. Although HNs are in themselves a valid and valued form of provision, as signalled by the salary behaviour of Scottish employers, they are not yet serving as a significant pathway into full cycle HE.

Gallacher (2002) has described the Scottish HE system as consisting of two parallel systems, which have evolved on a largely unplanned basis. The country's higher education system is distinguished by a high level of participation in short cycle higher education courses offered through further education colleges. Yet although this has led to considerable growth in participation, closer investigation suggests that those who enter HE in further education gain significantly fewer benefits as a result than do those who enter degree courses in universities. The most significant benefits to learners come directly from the acquisition of short cycle higher education qualifications, and not indirectly as a result of the opportunity to progress to full graduate status. As those who enter HE courses in FE are disproportionately recruited from the least advantaged backgrounds, current Scottish policy thus makes a limited contribution to increased social mobility and equity. Chapter 3 makes it clear that similar judgements can be made for the contribution of two-year college programmes in the USA.

Clearly, further research is required to explore the Scottish experience in considerably greater depth. Relatively little is known about employers' attitudes towards HN awards, and this chapter has had to make inferences based on the salaries that HN holders attract. However, it is not clear whether those who recruit HN holders do so because of the perceived merits of their specific qualification, or whether it is being used as a screening device. Salary differentials in the labour market of today are likely to reflect in part the individual's perceived achievements since gaining the award, but again there is no basis for judging the extent to which this might outweigh the direct impact of the qualification. Nor do we know whether employers' attitudes towards HNs are remaining constant at a time of considerable growth in the supply of HN holders. This area is therefore ripe for further investigation. At present, all we can say is that the current evidence on salary differentials confirms the anecdotal view of the value that Scottish employers place on short cycle awards.

Equally significant gaps remain in our knowledge in respect of equity and short cycle awards delivered in non-university settings. In particular, there is a strong case for mobilising longitudinal methods to track an individual's progression through and from short cycle HE courses delivered in FECs. At present, it looks as though such students quite explicitly face a second-class experience, and are likely to do so unless there are both appropriate mechanisms and the political will to secure greater equivalence and much more direct routes of progression between short cycle and full cycle HE in the college and university contexts. Moreover, this pattern also has implications for other attempts to develop HE in non-university settings. If streaming is so marked between two sectors as similar as further and higher education, what hope is there for securing equivalence and progression in respect of workplace learning and community-based learning?

Notes

1 The data in this figure come from SHEFC (2004) in respect of articulation rate, and follow the definition of articulation rate used

in that circular; for retention, I have used the main UK performance indicator rate in HEFCE (2003). While neither of these indicators is entirely satisfactory in itself, together they nonetheless make the point that student success rates and articulation rates are inversely correlated.

References

Caldwell, D. (2003) Scottish Higher Education: Character and provision. In T. Bryce and W. Humes (eds), *Scottish Education*, pp. 62–73. Edinburgh: Edinburgh University Press.

Connor, H., Tyers, C., Modood, T. and Hillage, J. (2004) *Why the Difference? A Closer Look at Higher Education Minority Ethnic Students and Graduates*, Research Report RR552. Sheffield: Department for Education and Skills.

Edwards, R. (1997) *Changing Places? Flexibility, Lifelong Learning and a Learning Society*. London: Routledge.

Gallacher, J. (2002) Articulation Links Between Further Education Colleges and Higher Education Institutions in Scotland. In M. Osborne, J. Gallacher and M. Murphy (eds), *A Research Review of FE/HE Links – A Report to the Scottish Executive Enterprise and Lifelong Learning Department*, pp. 4–16. Glasgow/Stirling: Centre for Research in Lifelong Learning.

Gallacher, J. (2003) *Higher Education in Further Education Colleges: The Scottish experience*. London: Council for Industry and Higher Education.

Gasteen, A. and Houston, J. (2003) *Scottish Further Education Qualifications: Employability and wage premia effects*. Stirling: SCOTECON.

Goodwin, L. L. (2002) *Resilient Spirits: Disadvantaged students making it at an elite university*. London, New York: Routledge Falmer.

H. M. Inspectors of Schools (1998) *Higher Education in Scottish Further Education Colleges*. Edinburgh: Scottish Office Education and Industry Department.

Higher Education Funding Council for England (2003) *Performance Indicators in Higher Education: 2000–01 and 2001–02*. Bristol: HEFCE

Humes, W. and Bryce, T. (2003) The Distinctiveness of Scottish Education. In T. Bryce and W. Humes (eds), *Scottish Education*, pp. 108–18. Edinburgh: Edinburgh University Press.

Hyland, T. and Merrill, B. (2003) *The Changing Face of Further Education: Lifelong learning, inclusion and community values in further education*, London: Routledge Falmer.

McLaurin, I. and Osborne, M. (2002) Data on transfer from FECs in Scotland to HEIs in Scotland. In M. Osborne, J. Gallacher and M. Murphy (eds), *A Research Review of FE/HE Links – A Report to the Scottish Executive Enterprise and Lifelong Learning Department*, pp. 111–38. Glasgow/Stirling: Centre for Research in Lifelong Learning,

MacLennan, A., Musselbrook, K. and Dundas, M. (2000) *Credit transfer at the FE/HE interface: Widening opportunities*. Edinburgh: Scottish Higher Education Funding Council.

Morgan-Klein, B. (2003) 'Scottish Higher Education and the FE–HE Nexus', *Higher Education Quarterly*, Vol. 57, No 4, pp. 338–54.

Morris, L. (1979) *Elusive Equality: The status of black Americans in higher education*. Washington DC: Howard University Press.

Parry, G. (2003) 'Mass Higher Education and the English: wherein the Colleges?', *Higher Education Quarterly*, Vol. 57, No 4, pp. 308–37.

Ramsden, B. (2003) *Review of the Initial Entry Rate into Higher Education*. London: Department for Education and Skills.

Scott, P. (2000) The Death of Mass Higher Education and the Birth of Lifelong Learning. In J. Field and M. Leicester (eds), *Lifelong Learning: Education across the lifespan*, pp. 29–42. London: Routledge Falmer.

Scottish Executive (2003a) *Life Through Learning Through Life: The lifelong learning strategy for Scotland*. Edinburgh: Stationery Office.

Scottish Executive (2003b) *Students in Higher Education in Scotland: 2001–02*, Edinburgh: Scottish Executive.

Scottish Executive (2003c) *A Framework for Higher Education in Scotland*. Edinburgh: Stationery Office.

Scottish Further Education Funding Council (SFEFC) (2000) *Qualification Aim by Outcome and Mode*, www.sfefc.ac.uk/content/sfefc/festats/factsfig/9900/FDG/tables.xls.

Scottish Higher Education Funding Council (2004) *Allocation of Funding to Support FE-HE Articulation 2003–05*. Edinburgh: SHEFC.

Scottish Qualifications Authority (SQA) (2003) *Annual Statistical Report 2002*. Glasgow: SQA.

Chapter 6

The educational divide: an economics perspective

Sandy Baum

Distressing gaps in educational attainment levels related to family income, race and ethnicity, and social class persist in both the USA and the UK despite the considerable resources – both financial and intellectual – that have been directed at the problem in recent decades. The failure of public policy to follow the prescriptions of social scientists surely contributes to the limited progress. Perhaps revisiting the theoretical approach of the relevant disciplines can provide both a clearer foundation for policy and a stronger array of recommendations aimed at reducing the role of higher education in perpetuating social inequalities. This paper addresses the questions of access and success in higher education from the perspective of an economist.

An economics approach to the educational divide

Few economists deeply involved in higher education policy discussions adhere strictly to the tenets of neoclassical economic theory with its emphasis on the efficiency of competitive markets and the optimality of unfettered market forces. The clear role of market imperfections, the obvious interaction of social, economic and political forces in determining educational opportunities and outcomes, and the social values most likely to lead researchers into this field of enquiry all dictate a broader approach. Nonetheless, most economists share a reliance on a set of theoretical tools that leads our analyses to differ considerably from those outside the discipline. Although without proper context they may lead down some unproductive paths, these tools allow considerable insight into the causes of and potential solutions to persistent educational inequality.

The most basic dichotomy in economics is between supply and demand. Although we do not usually think of universities and their students as producers and consumers, in a very real sense they are just that and this framework provides a useful perspective. Is the educational gap primarily a supply problem or a demand problem? The interaction of supply and demand determines who ends up consuming what, but it is useful to begin by thinking of the two blades of the scissors separately. After considering these two aspects of the market separately, including examining the role of choice in educational attainment, the discussion that follows turns to other economic concepts, including price discrimination and human capital formation. It then outlines some general policy implications emerging from the economic perspective on inequalities in higher education.

The supply side

Consider first the supply side. What are the goals of the providers of education? Generally not profit-making organisations, what are the outcomes universities hope to maximise? Are educational institutions designed to meet the needs of some segments of the population more than others? Is the number of places in colleges artificially restricted?

In order to think about the supply side of the equation, it is useful to think about the roles of both government and higher education institutions in making educational opportunities available. In the UK, separating these two players has not been so important historically, as both the funding and the provision of higher education have been almost exclusively the role of the national government through national agencies. In the USA, the system is more complex, with the state governments providing the bulk of the funding for public institutions, where about 80 per cent of college students are enrolled, the federal government providing portable subsidies to students, and a sizeable share of colleges and universities being private non-profit entities. For simplicity, this discussion focuses on the partnership relationships in the USA. However, proposed changes in the funding structure in the UK make it advisable to view institutions as separate players in both countries.

There are about 4,200 degree-granting post-secondary institutions in the United States. Seventeen hundred are public colleges or universities and 2,500 are private (US Department of Education, 2002, Table 243). The for-profit sector is growing rapidly, but enrolls only about four per cent of college students (The College Board, 2003). Obviously the profit motive underlying many models of economic behavior cannot explain the supply of educational services. This does not mean, however, either that the motivation is entirely altruistic or that economic concepts are irrelevant. Williams College economist Gordon Winston's characterisation of institutions as 'part church and part car dealer' (Winston, 2002) is apt. Colleges are charitable organisations because they almost always charge less for their services than it costs them to produce those services. They subsidise virtually all students through some combination of government funding and endowment or gifts from private philanthropic sources.

But no matter how charitable they would like to be and no matter how committed to educational opportunity they are, colleges and universities cannot survive if they are not financially sound. Striving for status in the presence of financial constraints has led US institutions to compete for students in ways that are clearly detrimental to efforts to equalise educational opportunities across socio-economic groups. Colleges and universities are diverting funds away from need-based aid for low-income students and from other institutional priorities in order to discount tuition for selected students who will increase net revenues and/or improve the school's academic profile and reputation. Even two-year public colleges in the USA, which have essentially open admissions and provide the foundation of access for low-income and non-traditional students, are allocating some funds to non-need-based grant aid.

This trend is clearly problematic in terms of equity. It is also inefficient, despite potential short-term institutional benefits. Subsidies can be efficient only if they change behavior. As discussed below, the more affluent students are, the less likely subsidies are to alter their choices. If the goal of subsidising students is to increase enrolments in higher education, then subsidies must be directed at those who would not otherwise enrol. Reducing financial barriers for those with the most constrained resources is the most effective route to increasing the population of students. Preventing individual institutions from competing with each other in ways that limit opportunities is not an easy task, particularly under the restrictions of US anti-trust laws. Perhaps highlighting the potential inefficiencies of this form of competition can provide a basis for more equitable and efficient enrolment and financing patterns.

The second supply question posed above relates to meeting the needs of only selected groups of enrolled students. If institutions prefer to enrol more affluent and better-prepared students, it is not unreasonable to expect them to be more hospitable to these students than to those who bring lesser personal, academic and financial resources to campus. Improving the success rate of students from lower socio-economic status (SES) backgrounds who do enrol in higher education requires careful scrutiny of the social and academic environments on campus, with an understanding that institutions are unlikely to adequately fulfil this responsibility without external incentives.

Because of enrolment priorities, restrictions on the number of places in higher education are likely to have their greatest impact on access for low SES students.

There are few supporters of explicitly designing policies to restrict the supply of university seats. But basic economic analysis points clearly to the relationship between artificially low prices and quantities supplied. Inadequate public funding of colleges and universities is a visible and increasing problem in both the USA and the UK. In any market, restricted inputs reduce the quantity supplied. In unfettered markets, the decline in the level of output is mitigated by increases in price, which make it possible for firms to produce more. If we impose price controls on firms – as is essentially the case in public higher education – the quantity supplied falls even more than it otherwise would (see Figure 6.1). In other words, forcing tuition to remain low without replacing the foregone funds is almost certain to exacerbate the access problem for those at the bottom of the queue.

Figure 6.1: Impact of price ceiling on quantity supplied

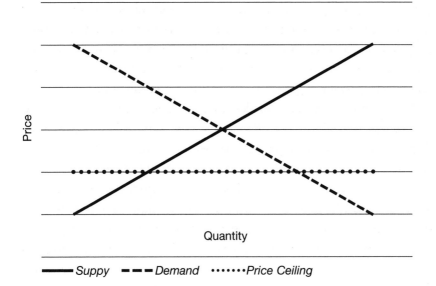

━━━ *Suppy* ━ ━ ━*Demand* •••••••*Price Ceiling*

The demand side

Thinking in terms of demand raises different questions. Are certain groups under-represented in higher education because they are not interested in participating, because they do not have the necessary academic preparation, or because they lack the ability to pay? How do students and potential students make their decisions about enrolling and persisting in college? Do they rationally weigh the costs and benefits of education? Do they compare the lifetime earnings streams they can expect with and without a higher degree? How important are disparate social norms and other non-pecuniary aspects of educational choices? Perhaps most fundamentally, is it constructive to think of the relatively low participation rates of particular demographic groups as choices at all?

Demand, in the economic sense of the word, incorporates two basic components. First, do people 'want' the product? Will they benefit from purchasing/consuming it? What priority do they place on it relative to other things they might buy? Included here are all of the very real questions about social norms, expectations and academic preparation. The perception that college is out of reach financially certainly affects the expectations and preparation levels of high-school graduates. So the price of college – and the subsidies available to help pay that price – do contribute to this aspect of demand, but other factors may be even more central. Lower costs of attendance and increased subsidies to college students will not, on their own, remove these non-pecuniary barriers to educational attainment.

The second component of demand, complementing the preference for college, is ability to pay. Economists speak of 'effective demand' – demand that is backed up by the necessary funds. We know that significant gaps in college enrolment and completion rates exist according to economic circumstances among students at comparable levels of academic achievement. In the USA, almost all students in the highest quartile for both academic achievement and income go to college. Among those with the same academic qualifications who are in the lowest family income quartile, only about three-quarters enrol. This is about the same as the proportion of the most affluent group who test in the lowest quartile who enrol (US Department of Education, 1997, p. 64).

Moreover, there is considerable empirical evidence indicating that unlike upper- and middle-income students, those from low-income families are quite price-sensitive in their decisions about whether or not to continue their education after high school. It takes many thousands of dollars to affect an affluent student's decision about whether to attend Stanford or the University of California. An interesting public policy example comes from Massachusetts, where the Governor has recently proposed a new state grant programme that would grant free tuition (about $2,000) to top test scorers. Estimates of the cost of the programme confidently rely on the knowledge that only a tiny number of the affluent students who score well on the tests in question will actually decide to enrol in the state university as a result of receiving this subsidy. Certainly no special financial incentives are required to convince them to continue their education after high school. Price matters a lot to some students. It matters little to others.

The preference and resource components of demand are not entirely separable. Just as the perception of inability to pay for college may contribute to the failure to prepare academically, willingness to make sacrifices to pay for college is frequently a prerequisite for amassing the necessary resources. This is true not only of saving in advance, but of willingness to borrow. For a majority of students in both the USA and the UK – and in an increasing number of other countries – successful participation in higher education requires borrowing. Whether the borrowing is characterised as debt or as the postponement of tuition charges until after graduation, the willingness to incur this long-term financial obligation has essentially become a necessity for being able to pay for college. In other words, ability to pay for college cannot, from a pragmatic perspective, be defined solely in terms of current available resources. Altering attitudes about sacrificing other consumption in order to take responsibility for personal educational priorities has the potential to ease the financing problem.

Choice?

A fundamental premise of standard economic analysis of demand is that economic agents make rational choices. For consumers, this means maximising utility by assuring that the last dollar spent on any good or service generates as much benefit as the last dollar spent on every other commodity. In order to make these rational choices, consumers must have perfect information about the options available to them and must be able to predict the benefits they will receive. The choices available are, of course, constrained by resource limitations. An increase in income allows a consumer to purchase more goods and services and to reach a higher level of utility.

Economists rarely ask people about their preferences. Instead, they rely on revealed preferences – they look at what people actually buy at given prices to determine the value they place on things. Economists also refrain from making judgements about consumer choices – at least *qua* economists. That is, as an economist, it is inappropriate to say that students *should* be more willing to sacrifice current consumption in order to participate in higher education. Consumers weigh the expected costs and benefits of their options and make utility-maximising choices.

This economic approach raises two fundamental questions. One is whether the conditions for rational consumer choice exist in the market for higher education and the second is whether the constraints faced by some segments of the population are so severe as to prevent the decision not to go to college – or not to persist in earning a degree – from being considered a choice in any meaningful sense of the word.

A decision about college participation can be 'rational' only if potential students are fully aware of how much college costs, of how much they will actually have to pay to go to college, of the different alternatives available to them, and of the pay-off to college in terms of future earnings. This awareness cannot develop at the time of high school graduation, when the college decision is apparently made. It has to occur much earlier, when students have time to acquire the necessary preparation. Both parents and students must have the information so that families can engage in long-term planning and make wise choices together.

This framework for analysing individual choice carries potential risks for college access efforts in that it could lead some observers to the conclusion that differential levels of educational attainment are largely the reflection of differences in individual characteristics and preferences. It obscures the social context in which decisions are made and suggests that individuals make optimal personal choices, subject to existing constraints.

But the framework also serves to highlight key factors that limit educational opportunities. Consumers can only make rational choices if they have adequate information. Potential students must understand the role of both grant and loan aid in reducing the financial burden of college and they must understand from an early age that it is the net price they will be required to pay, not the published tuition and fee levels, that is most relevant to their options. They must be aware of the long-term return on investment in higher education, and the likely costs over a lifetime of not acquiring this education.

Policy makers, institutions, and others with responsibility for setting prices and allocating subsidies must consider the implications of the differential budget constraints facing potential students. Budget constraints so low that they effectively eliminate successful participation in higher education from individual choice sets should be the primary target of public policy.

Price discrimination

The policy of granting need-based aid and price discounts based on other criteria, such as athletic skill or academic merit, to individual students, is a classic example of the practice dubbed 'price discrimination' by economists. Price discrimination involves selling similar goods or services to different customers at different prices. This practice may involve either differentiating among two or more groups of consumers or charging each individual consumer exactly the price corresponding to their own demand. The former is more common, and is illustrated by, for example, higher airline prices for business travellers than for holiday makers. The guiding principle is that it is profit-maximising for firms to charge higher prices to consumers who are less price sensitive. The practice of basing subsidies for college on individual financial circumstances is an example of the less common price discrimination at the individual level, facilitated by the requirement that applicants for subsidies submit personal financial information. Price discrimination can increase profits because it allows firms to charge higher prices to customers willing to pay those prices, without losing customers for whom prices must be lower. But it may also be both efficient and equitable from a social perspective.

In markets that are not perfectly competitive because they are characterised by product differentiation or some other factor generating a degree of monopoly power, the market price tends to be higher than the actual marginal cost of producing an extra unit of output. This means that some consumers are excluded even though they are willing and able to pay enough to cover the cost of the extra output. The marginal cost of adding an extra student to the university population may be very low, but since the actual tuition cost is higher than this marginal cost, students with the most limited resources are excluded if they are not charged lower prices. Even though the marginal benefit of educating the student would be greater than the marginal cost, the student does not get an education. This is inefficient.

It is also inequitable, because it is the low-income students who are most likely to be deprived of educational opportunities.

Charging a price to all consumers that is low enough to allow those with very low ability and/or willingness to pay to enter the market makes it impossible for the supplier to cover the costs of production. For-profit firms would likely go out of business. Colleges and universities, forced to price in this manner, find it impossible to maintain quality, in addition to being forced to restrict supply, as explained above in the discussion of price controls.

Recognition of both the problems of artificially imposed restrictions on prices and the positive aspects of differential pricing systems for consumers has important policy implications. It leads to arguments favouring charging tuition levels high enough to provide adequate resources for institutions while assuring adequate subsidies for students with insufficient resources to pay those tuition levels.

Human capital

Education is an investment that increases students' productive capacity and earning power over their lifetimes. In other words, it creates human capital. The return to this human capital accrues partially to the individual student and partially to society as a whole. The social benefits provide the foundation for arguments about the efficiency of public investment in higher education. The private benefits provide the basis for the equity and efficiency of individuals contributing to the financing of their own education. The more a college education increases earnings potential, the more students should be willing to pay for that education. In other words, an understanding of human capital, of the role of education in increasing an individual's human capital, and of the role of human capital in determining earnings, can help people to evaluate what is a reasonable amount to pay for education.

The idea of education as an investment that pays off over a lifetime also makes it easier to explain why it is logical to save and to borrow to finance higher education. The concept of borrowing to finance investment in physical capital is well established. Few people would think it advisable to avoid all capital investment unless they have the savings necessary to buy the plant and equipment they need to operate a business. They understand that the loans can be paid off through the revenues generated by the capital investment. This same reasoning can be applied to the investment in human capital.

It is not easy to engage in reasoned conversations about the appropriateness of student borrowing in the atmosphere of crisis fuelled by US headlines about students drowning in debt; it is even more difficult in the politically charged British environment. The need for both countries to increase their capacity to educate a larger proportion of students from disadvantaged backgrounds is urgent. It is, therefore, imperative that public and political understanding of the merits of students bearing a reasonable portion of the cost of higher education be increased. So long as participation in higher education is not evenly distributed across income classes, and so long as the return to the human capital generated by higher education remains high, it will be both equitable and efficient for the financing burden to be shared by the public treasury and the private beneficiaries.

Access and success

As we make progress in increasing access to higher education, the difference between access and success becomes more and more evident. We are better at getting students into college than we are at providing the financial, academic and social support necessary for many of these students to persist in earning degrees. The proportion of US high-school graduates from the lowest family income quintile who entered college immediately increased from 43 per cent in 1981 to 47 per cent in 1991 and 57 per cent in 2001 (College Board, 2003, Figure 11). But a third of the students who enrolled in college in 1995 – and 19 per cent of those who enrolled with the stated intention of earning a bachelor's degree – were no longer enrolled three years later (NCES, 2001, Table 27.1).

Successful progress to degree depends on a variety of factors, including finances, academic preparation and motivation. Of particular importance in the context of a discussion of the insights contributed by economic analysis is the unique nature of education as a commodity.

Entering college is, in many ways, analogous to buying any other good or service. But in most other cases, the producer's role is complete once the product is purchased. This is not the case for education, where ongoing interaction between the producer and the consumer is required.

The relevance for financing strategies is that lowering the entry price of college may successfully increase the proportion of high-school graduates who begin post-secondary education. But this progress is not sufficient to assure meaningful increases in educational attainment. Adequate institutional resources are a prerequisite for creating an environment in which non-traditional and marginally prepared students can thrive. Focusing only on the price of admission is likely to create false promises.

Policy implications

While the issue of the gaps in educational attainment across socio-economic classes is generally couched in terms of equity, it also clearly represents significant inefficiency. Education increases labour force productivity, reduces poverty and dependence on social welfare programmes, and increases civic participation. Even in the absence of a high priority on equity and increasing opportunities, these social benefits justify considerable public investment in making higher education accessible to all who can benefit from it.

The importance of public subsidies does not mean that holding the sticker price of college to the lowest level possible is necessarily the best policy for promoting either equity or efficiency. In the absence of increasingly generous institutional appropriations, keeping the price low for all students restricts the capacity of educational institutions. It is low-income students who are most likely to be shut out. Direct subsidies to students can differentiate between students with financial need and those more affluent students whose educational opportunities are not dependent on public subsidies. General subsidies, in the form of low tuition for all students, do not allow this sort of equitable and efficient targeting.

Charging a higher general price but providing ample individualised subsidies for students on the basis of ability to pay has the potential to increase educational attainment at the lower end of the income distribution. This favourable outcome is, however, dependent on changing public perceptions.

The arguments for targeted subsidies are particularly difficult to promote in the UK, but they are also disturbingly absent from much of the public discussion in the USA. Opposition to the reform of higher education financing in the UK has been couched in terms of preserving access to universities for low-income students. Criticism of rising tuition levels and of proposals to increase federal student loan limits in the US are more focused on affordability for the middle-class. In both countries, the emphasis on the sticker price of college and the lack of awareness of the role of need-based grant aid actually threaten access to education in an era of competing priorities for limited public funds.

Just as lack of understanding of differential pricing is a barrier to rational policies, if people had better information about the long-term earnings premiums attributable to higher levels of education – and better information about the family-of-origin socio-economic status of those who do and those who do not go to college – they probably would be more reluctant to advocate relying so heavily on general subsidies. Support for public policies that rely partially on student debt to expand educational opportunities would be more widespread and there would be less danger of 'sticker shock' discouraging enrolment.

Economic arguments for the equity and efficiency of shared financing responsibility suggest that the perpetuation of inequality by the education system is more likely to be mitigated by a policy targeting subsidies at those who need them most, than by a policy that diffuses the benefits, leaving the price out of reach for the neediest students and leaving institutions with insufficient resources to provide quality educational experiences for a diverse student body.

References

National Center for Education Statistics (2001) *The Condition of Education*. Student Effort and Educational Progress: Student Persistence and Progress. Indicator 27.

National Center for Education Statistics (2002) *Digest of Education Statistics 2002*. Washington: US Department of Education.

Smith, T., Young, B., Bae, Y., Choy, S. P. and Alsalam, N. (1997) *The Condition of Education 1997*. NCES 97–388. National Center for Education Statistics. Washington: US Department of Education.

The College Board (2003) *Trends in College Pricing 2003*. New York: The College Board.

US Census Bureau (2002). *Statistical Abstract of the United States*. www.census.gov/ prod/2002pubs/01statab/income.pdf

US Department of Education (1997) *Condition of Education*. Washington DC: US Government Printing Office.

US Department of Education (2002) *Digest of Education Statistics, Table 243*. Washington DC: US Government Printing Office.

Winston, Gordon (2002) 'Statement of Gordon Winston, Professor of Economics, Williams College, October 2, 2002, Committee on Education and the Workforce.' US House of Representatives. http://edworkforce.house.gov/ hearings/ 107th/fc/collcost100302/ winston.htm

Chapter 7

What price inclusion? Debates and discussions about learning and teaching to widen participation in higher education

Mary Stuart

Governments across the world argue that increasing the diversity of the higher education (HE) student population is vital to their economic competitiveness and to social cohesion (Delors, 1997). Increasingly higher education institutions are expected to contribute to the development of society itself, not just the development of academic knowledge.As the Association of Commonwealth Universities (ACU) points out:

> A university's mission must thus be much wider than perpetuating the life of scholarship for its own sake. The world depends increasingly on universities for knowledge, prosperity, health and policy thinking. Universities are thus required to become engines of development for people, institutions and democracy in general (ACU, 2001: i)

However, in the British media there is a debate about the value of increasing the number of graduates, which suggests that social inclusion in HE is still a contested idea (THES, 2004c). For those who argue that widening participation is necessary to social development, like the ACU, there is a recognition that widening participation in HE is costly. This perspective grows out of an understanding that widening access is only one part of widening *participation*. Successful inclusion of under-represented groups in HE requires a substantial engagement in pedagogy, not just in outreach programmes. Increasing the diversity of the student population increases the diversity of learning experience, the diversity of student demand for curricula and the diversity of life experiences of the student population. The student life-cycle model (Layer, Stuart and Srivastava, 2003) suggests that widening participation requires a long-term engagement from before a student thinks of applying to HE and beyond their graduation into employment. The costs and risks are not just for institutions but for the students themselves who risk a great deal to move from one set of social values where HE is not a part of their community or family experience, to another where HE is part of a rite of passage for the professional classes.

The full spectrum of HE provision includes HE provided by higher education institutions (HEIs), specialist colleges and further education colleges (FECs). Pedagogy in FECs is somewhat different from that in HEIs. HE in further education has always been closer to its local communities and has traditionally been closer to the employer community as well, and here there is a greater engagement with learning that takes account of student diversity (Parry and Thompson, 2002). HE in further education has had a very successful past in Scotland with more mixed experience in England. Current British government policy has particularly highlighted the role of further education colleges in delivering first-cycle HE to enable greater social inclusion in HE. Funding bodies, as well as institutions, are grappling with these issues, but in this chapter I suggest that engagement must take account of other wider social factors and include partnerships with potential learners and their communities.

This chapter examines the debate about widening participation and learning and teaching practice. It sets out a number of different perspectives on learning and teaching in HE and student diversity, examining the relationship between these different perspectives and the purpose of HE, as well as discussing necessary connections to compulsory education practice and the experiences and attitudes of the so-called new student groups themselves.

It argues that successful social inclusion in HE will require a new engagement with participation – participation that includes many players, students and their communities, schools and teachers and employers, as well as those directly working in HE to transform the academy to meet the challenges of twenty-first century social life (ACU, 2001). The costs of this sort of transformation are substantial, not only in financial terms but socially and personally. However, the chapter concludes that if widening participation agenda does not transform learning and teaching practice and does not enable students to succeed in their studies, the costs to society will be much greater. I begin by setting out the challenge of widening participation.

Perpetual exclusion

Looking back at policy documents in England produced at the start of the twentieth century, one might be forgiven for thinking that they were written as part of the case for widening participation a century later. McNicols (2004) points out that many of the same debates are evident. The concern about working class under-representation, the needs of the society and the social benefits of higher-level study are all evident in the documents. Despite many successes in widening access to HE through the century, particularly for women, there remains an intractable problem for working class communities' participation in HE and indeed in education itself (Taylor and Cameron, 2002). In this chapter, I focus on widening participation and social inclusion in HE for students from poorer backgrounds, acknowledging that in the UK there are other groups who are also marginalised in HE, such as disabled students, but to examine all excluded groups goes beyond the scope of this chapter. Evidence continues to grow to highlight that the expansion of HE has sufficiently increased the participation of students from lower socio-economic backgrounds in the UK (Bynner and Joshi, 2002) or across the world, even where there are higher participation rates. Osborne points out that:

> . . . despite a plethora of policy initiatives and the use of a variety of interventions, there is continuing under-representation of certain traditionally excluded groups in these five countries (Finland, England, France, Australia and Canada).

And

> . . . a strong economic rationale associated with competition for students, institutional survival and reduction of unit costs underpins many forms of provision and this rather than equity often guides practices (my brackets) (Osborne, 2003, p. 48).

Increasing the diversity of the student community in an HEI through business need, is not necessarily negative. However, doing so does not necessarily translate into changing learning and teaching practice, because the reasoning is to ensure student numbers entering not necessarily student success in completion.

Statistics suggest that in Britain only about 40 per cent of the workforce is educated to level 3, the threshold for HE level learning, compared to Germany where the percentage is 75 per cent (Steedman, 2001). Evidence of participation in the UK suggests that compared to other European Union countries, Britain has the second lowest participation rate of any country (Office of National Statistics, 2001). However, staying on at 17, while a considerable problem to be addressed, is not the only question that needs to be examined. If young people in the UK did stay on and take on higher-level study, it is also vital that they are able to complete their studies successfully. It is a false dichotomy to separate access from participation: rather I argue that the two areas are inextricably linked. Student success requires an understanding of the barriers to access as much as to participation.

Grappling in the half-light – current perspectives

In recent years in HE in the UK there have been moves to attempt to engage with a more holistic view of learning and teaching in HE. However, widening participation in HE for under-represented groups includes a variety of different groups and changing practice in HE teaching is varied. For example, examining the websites of the learning and teaching subject centres for HE in the UK, it is clear that changing learning and teaching practice in HE for widening participation has been dominated by the need to comply with changes stemming from the Disability Discrimination Act, more than widening participation for any other socially excluded group. However, it is the case that many changes to curriculum and teaching practice for disabled students will be of benefit to all student groups. In a recent study of HE 'widening participation' strategies, Layer, Stuart and Srivastava (2003) found that institutions were increasingly engaging with the learning and teaching debate:

> In response to students' changing needs Higher Education Institutions (HEIs) have over the last 15 years developed more flexible approaches to learning and are offering greater choice and flexibility with respect to attendance, mode of study and levels of engagement. (2003, p. 7)

These issues are not only being addressed in the UK. Osborne (2003) highlights a similar change in French and Australian 'widening participation' initiatives:

> (More recently in France) . . . new initiatives tend to be holistic, as there are worries that the expansion will lead to failure and dropout. An emphasis has been placed on universities working directly with secondary schools, orientation programmes upon entry to university, developing study skills, tutorial provision and more pre- and post-entry guidance and support. (p. 48)

> . . . in Australia ... teaching-learning initiatives that include more holistic approaches to development of curricula at HE level. [Universities are

159

developing] three components in the teaching-learning framework. In the first year, there would involve a structure designed around student needs and the university providing enhanced learning support for commencing students to facilitate effective transition to tertiary study. (p. 52)

Underpinning these changes are different attitudes to increasing student diversity. These perspectives can be divided broadly into two camps. There are those that suggest new student groups need to develop the skills to succeed in the HE environment and that 'remedial teaching', once in HE, is necessary. This response is common in the UK in many science disciplines where students often seem to be ill-prepared for the HE curriculum. This perspective is not always framed in terms such as 'remedial', and may focus on skill support (Rhodes, Bill, Biscomb, and Nevil, 2002). The taken-for-granted here is that the HE curriculum is appropriate as it stands and that, in order to secure standards, students need to fit into this curriculum with the understanding that they may need additional support. Some who hold this perspective see the students as deficient as Bowl points out:

> The language of higher education was assumed to be neutral by those within the system. If a student did not understand what was required, she felt that this would be construed as her failure to meet (unspecified) academic standards, rather than a failure on the part of the institution to help the student to comprehend and evaluate the worth of academic language. (Bowl, 2003, p. 139)

On the other hand, 'widening participation' practitioners and social inclusion protagonists argue that the higher education curriculum, teaching practice and the HE institutions themselves have to change to meet the needs of the new economy and need to recognise that increasing the diversity of student background can itself create; 'a dynamic culture embodying a multiplicity of sub-cultures, each imbued with their own discourses, literacies and practices' (Lawrence, 2002, p. 220). This is a more transformative model of participation in HE, one that suggests a more root and branch evaluation of how HE engages with its student communities. This approach is a more radical agenda for the future of higher-level study and challenges some of the embedded values of the academy. Protagonists of this perspective often suggest new forms of HE study, in terms of either mode or curricula which, in its most radical form, would lead to the redesign of HE provision itself.

However, both of these different perspectives tend to focus on the HE context and seldom consider the wider context in which students develop, their schooling or their community experience, nor does it tend to evaluate the role of HE in society itself. Equally, debates in Britain about pedagogy tend to focus on the British context, and increasingly, more locally, in Wales, Scotland, Northern Ireland and England. It is these contextual factors which will influence student achievement and successful pedagogy will work with these social factors. In the rest of this chapter I will discuss these contextual issues, before returning to the question of pedagogical approaches. I begin this discussion of contextual factors by examining the role of schooling for many students from lower socio-economic family backgrounds.

'Rust belt' learning

> The global rust belt trails around the United Kingdom, through parts of Europe, Canada and the United States, and through Australia and New Zealand – an indelible blemish on the economic complexion of some of the wealthiest countries in the world. (Thomson, 2002, p. 26)

This evocative description of post-industrial society points to the heart of the problem of social exclusion. Capitalist society offers much but only delivers a 'rough justice'. In the globalised world of post-industrial societies, neighbourhoods are distinguished by indices of wealth and poverty. The 'rust belt' is an area where industrial work has failed and been replaced by a range of post-industrial employment, often more insecure and often where the gender balance of work has altered (Massey and Jess, 1995). In these areas, alongside unequal access to housing stock, health care and other social facilities, school provision is differentiated. It is not just a question of resources but the environment in which the school is located. These geographic distinctions create quite different types of school experience whether or not the same curricula is studied, as Thomson points out:

> Regardless of whether socio-economic contexts and circumstances are acknowledged or not, their effects are integral to everyday life in disadvantaged schools. Teachers contend daily with myriad contextually produced mundane and routine frustrations, achievements, sadnesses and micro-politics and struggle to find the words to explain how it is that relentlessly focusing on learning is easier to say than to do. (2002: 17)

The culture of such school environments is rooted in the context of the communities in which the school is sited. Schools in poorer neighbourhoods often have to engage in activities to support students and their families because there is no one else to offer this support. Teachers act as social workers, lawyers and health care professionals, not only as educators. Learning itself can come quite low down on the agenda because of the social climate in which the children exist:

> It is not uncommon for disadvantaged schools to spend much of their staff meeting time on matters that are primarily concerned with order – yard safety ... changing the drugs policy and so on. There is a considerable apparatus for, and expenditure of resources on, the development and maintenance of order.

> Children who are hungry, tired or ill have less energy for schoolwork, and working with them on such matters inevitably reduces the time allocated to the curriculum. (Thomson, 2002, p. 48)

These environments create a cycle of deprivation from which it is difficult to escape and difficult for educators to manage. In the league tables of schooling, despite the 'value added measure', schools with these difficulties are set alongside those operating in middle-class areas. Schools are judged in Britain as successful or failing in terms of school effectiveness but as Fielding (2001) notes, school effectiveness policies are too functional to develop all aspects of the students. He says:

> Its thin, measurement driven notion of schooling too easily marginalizes concerns of wider, more profound aspirations for the development of persons; and education itself is refashioned in ways that make the call for community seem weak, undemanding and vague. (p. 413)

In other words the schools operating in these communities have to engage with the social problems of the communities themselves, and the culture of narrow measurement cannot take account of this work. All of these factors are seldom spelt out in the literature on widening participation, but are important in trying to examine how students who manage to make it through to HE can succeed. It is likely that students studying in troubled schools will have found their own learning strategies, often despite the school and their peers (not necessarily despite the teachers). Equally, schools in poor neighbourhoods seldom have additional resources, limiting the breath of the curriculum, sometimes even lacking adequate resources for teachers and materials. In thinking about pedagogies for greater student diversity it is important to have some sort of contextual understanding of the learning experiences of students. No student arrives in HE as a blank slate, yet the HE curriculum tends to assume that student arrive 'prepared', as if there is a simple equation which can measure their preparedness.

Creating student success must start from the perspective of the student building the curriculum from their starting point. As well as schooling and neighbourhood, it is important to have some understanding of the 'new' student groups' lifestyles. Many lecturers in HE are far removed in age and life experience from students who are now entering HE. It is to this question of student lifestyle and experience that I now turn.

Life in the twenty-first century – a risky business

Social theorists such as Beck (1992) and Giddens (1991) argue that in a globalised world individuals increasingly find themselves subject to balancing risks in their daily lives. Part of the rhetoric of choice implies responsibility for risk; the State is rolled back and as it does so, individuals, particularly poorer groups in society, have to bear personal risks that previously had been the responsibility of the community. For many young people this can be a kind of liberation – freedom from elders and others who have power over their lives. However, growing up in this climate creates considerable insecurity, where often traditional relationships are destroyed, as Miles points out:

> Risk has apparently become central to our social lives precisely because of the move towards a global society. We are liberated from the constraints of local community but at one and the same time are bereft of traditional forms of protection and support mechanisms. (2000, p. 55)

In poorer neighbourhoods in post-industrial Britain there are few anchors. There are few 'jobs for life' and work identities are insecure as notions of 'community' differ within neighbourhoods and cultures. Ahier, Beck and Moore (2003) found in their study of HE students that perceptions of the civic have almost disappeared among young people. However, they found that these young people were concerned and interested in society at a more personal level. Young students were more concerned about their own group and those that they knew rather than the abstract 'society' or 'community' at large. Being young in Britain today often means living on the street and only sleeping at home. In a recent study of young working class people in Newcastle, researchers examined how social networks evolved:

> In effect, 'going out' represents the equivalent of 'community' to these young people, and as such is arguably not hedonistic at all, but rather reflects a deep-seated need to belong in an ever changing world ... young people were willing to undergo debt and family conflict in order to retain their group solidarity that 'going out' provided them with. (Miles, 2000, p. 104)

In an ever increasingly risky world, finding some sense of belonging becomes more and more important. This is a further development on the issues raised by Thomson in her study of schooling and school children, where family breakdown created kids on the street as 'trouble' (Thomson, 2002, p. 68). She argues that schoolchildren who are defined as being 'at risk' in this way, take on the identity of being 'at risk' (ibid. 2002, p. 66) or what Miles suggests are 'alternative careers' (Miles, 2000, p. 43). In this context, higher education study is seen to be part of another world of conformity and seems like something that is 'not for us' (McGivney, 1990; Meadows, 2001). Identity formation is itself more risky as young people without clear, although limited, pathways have to 'make-up' who they are (Giddens, 1991). As Rustin (2000) points out:

> Contemporary theorists of individualisation (Giddens, 1991; Beck, 1992) argue that modern society is giving a new importance to individuals. Where earlier agrarian and industrial societies provided social scripts, which most individuals were expected to follow, contemporary societies throw more responsibility on to individuals to choose their own identities. Social structures-classes, extended families, occupational communities, long-term employment within a firm which formerly provided strong frames for identity, grow weaker. Simultaneously, society exposes individuals to bombardments of information, alternative versions of how life might be lived, and requires of individuals that they construct an 'authentic' version of themselves, making use of the numerous identity-props which consumer-society makes available. (p. 33)

Those that do progress to HE have a very limited view of their own engagement, in order to maintain their hard-won identity. Archer et al., (2003) indicate that working class students, especially male students, draw:

> . . . clear boundaries between themselves and the middle class institution, positioning themselves as able to benefit from participation while not belonging to, or feeling ownership of, the institution. As . . . a black male student suggested, in order to 'allow' university to change him, he intended to adopt the same strategy as his friends, whereby 'they go through university, uni doesn't go through them. (p. 177)

This perspective is very far removed from the current value judgements made in HE about the experience of learning and provides some significant challenges to pedagogy. Archer et al. (2003) found that students were making active choices to remain distant from the institution as they continued to feel that the HE environment was alien. They found that this perspective was particularly prevalent among working-class male students. They point out that University study:

> . . . could 'interfere' with the maintenance of these powerful (masculine) identities, for example by removing men from spheres of work in which identities are produced and reducing their 'masculine capital' within an arena where middle-class men exercise greater power/competency, (p. 182)

The theory that working-class identities remain strong against the perceived identity of an HE graduate or student is further borne out by other studies such as Tett (2000), who also suggests that working-class students do not want to lose their class allegiance. Studies on mature students' writing practices in HE also confirm some of these findings, especially in relation to identity formation as students attempt to make sense of their experience in HE.

Studies that examine student writing suggest that developing academic writing skills can have a significant effect on the self-identity of the students (Ivanic, 1993; Stuart, 1999; Burke, 2002). Writing academically requires writing differently and for these students it becomes a challenge to their way of life, their history and who they are. The rite of passage to becoming a successful academic writer is one that, for many students without the cultural capital to simply 'know' what is required, is painful and emotionally challenging.

If this is the case, it suggests that the add-on skills support model to enable students to succeed may only be useful for some students, and instead, HE level study itself needs transforming and repositioning as less class-biased. It at least suggests that teachers in HE need to be aware of the complexity that they are dealing with in engaging with students who 'are not like them'. This form of contradiction produces potential conflicts within which educationalists and young people themselves become caught. These issues point to a need for debates on learning and teaching to think beyond the classroom and beyond the academy and to construct a more holistic view of students, and potential students, if there is ever to be an effective engagement with success for student learning. Of course where there are deficits in student knowledge, or skill, these should be corrected, but this model should not be used as an excuse to maintain the status quo. HE, perhaps more than other forms of education, must engage with current and future realities, including changing student realities and identities. Frand (2000) points out that the mindsets of students have changed as society has changed. He argues that most academics are operating in an 'industrial mindset' whereas the new students are operating in an 'information-age' mindset. He identifies ten characteristics of the information-age mindset, particularly highlighting the compression of time, the ubiquitous nature of connectivity, the intolerance of waiting, and a trial and error culture rather than reflection which throws manuals away, but which is far more interactive. This means that teachers and lecturers need to understand the changing nature of the student body but equally, the institutional context in which they work is important to enabling engagement with new student groups, and the next section discusses the challenges for the HEIs themselves.

Mixed missions and institutional challenges

Johnston (2003) points out that widening participation is risky for HE institutions themselves:

> Higher education institutions face risks ... accepting, accommodating and working with diverse types of student, changing culture and curriculum, being pilloried for offering 'Mickey Mouse' degrees, not to mention the vagaries and distortions of government funding. (p.5)

Taking this point further, Watson sets out a challenge for HE. He sees current policy in England as placing contradictory demands on the sector and suggests that further thinking should be done on the competing demands of widening access, mission convergence and institutional financial stability (Watson, 2002). One of roles of HE is to support social inclusion but there are key challenges if all institutions are expected to tackle all aspects of the social purpose of HE. Brown and Piatt (2001) highlight that funding for widening participation did not sufficiently compensate for the costs involved. While the higher education funding councils across the UK have attempted to address this using a variety of different means, it is still the case that HEIs having widening participation as their particular mission are disadvantaged (THES, 2004a). Equally for FECs, especially in England, there are significant risks in taking on HE level work in their institution, risks related to attracting students in a climate when demand remains flat, as well as resource and quality risks. In many ways these risks are, for FECs and HEIs who see widening participation as their main mission, a continuation of the difficulties of rust-belt schools as described by Thomson. It is therefore vital that society as a whole accepts that tackling social exclusion is not simply the task of one group of institutions, but needs to be part of a combined effort, as Thomson (2002) clearly illustrates:

> . . . education policy cannot be separated from other public policies and that working for social justice is inevitably linked to working for economic justice and work to eliminate the new and old geographies of distinction. (p. 190)

It is therefore unreasonable for institutions themselves to have to bear the whole risk. The issues of social inclusion need to be seen as a whole social policy where there are deep interconnections between different services, employers and the communities and individuals in which these institutions are working. Any search for excellence in learning and teaching at higher-level study must work from the premise that universities and other educational environments cannot be separated from the rest of society and society cannot separate itself from these institutions. To take this argument further, if all social institutions do not engage with the problems of exclusion and attempt to create more equality in provision then, as Field points out, 'the learning society will continue to generate ever greater inequality and exclusion, and become even more unstable' (Field, 2000, p. 150). Archer et al. (2003) also make this point when they say:

> Strategies aimed at widening participation will need to be located within numerous sites, such as schools, colleges, workplaces, community groups and universities, and should be linked into numerous social, educational and welfare policy agendas with the aim of redistributing power and privileges. (p. 201)

In the international context the same point is made of social policy in Australia (Thomson, 2002) and the USA (Apple, 1990). In other words, while the curriculum must engage with the students and their backgrounds to ensure success, and while it is imperative that there is partnership between different social groups and agencies, higher education, or indeed, education itself, cannot be expected to deal with all broader social issues. The British Labour Government's cry in 1997, that 'education, education, education' was the answer to social exclusion is therefore only partially valid. Once the broader context of 'new' student groups is acknowledged it is clear that further work needs to be done to create an environment where students from diverse backgrounds can feel at home to benefit from their study and it is to the question of teaching environments that I now turn.

Who speaks, who listens and who knows? Teaching and learning practice in HE

Higher education teaching and learning practice in Britain remains unprofessionalised. Despite Dearing's plea for a professional standing for HE teaching (Dearing, 1997) and the introduction of the HE Academy, and its predecessor the Institute for Learning and Teaching in Higher Education (ILTHE), teaching remains a lesser calling than research in an HEI. The mission of HE colleges on the other hand, particularly values and rewards excellence in teaching; however, the ethos of the academy and the emphasis of research selectivity has encouraged academics to move their teaching to higher levels of HE study leaving first-level teaching to part-time teaching assistants who have less power and less status in the institution (THES, 2004b). As Bowl (2003) points out:

> If teaching comes low down on the list of priorities, the teaching of first-year students is likely to be given even lower status. It is less likely to enable the lecturer to talk about their own research interests and carries even less symbolic capital than other undergraduate teaching. (p. 142)

This environment means that consideration of student need is often marginalised and that discussions of teaching practice remain the domain of individuals, rather than being fully embedded in taken-for-granted work practice in HE. The low status of teaching must be addressed before further progress can be made on changing learning and teaching practice. While many policy initiatives implemented by the funding councils and within institutions are working to address this, the woeful membership numbers of the ILTHE, as well as their institutional location, indicates that we have not yet got this issue right.

Within institutions there are many 'taken for granted' practices that go unchallenged. Bourdieu (1984) points out that educational establishments present a particular cultural atmosphere or 'Habitus'. He suggests that the environment created by particular teaching practices, which are known and common to those who have prior family experience of HE, create an uneven playing field for others to whom the rules and taken-for-granteds are not explained. Bowl (2003) expands:

> The habitus related to educational practices and policies may be unthinking, taken for granted, habitual. It could be argued that this explains the apparent contradiction between the institutional language which speaks of inclusion, and educational experiences which appear to exclude . . . It might also provide an explanatory framework for the apparent lack of significant change in institutional practices to take account of the rhetoric. (p. 125)

This suggests an unequal access to knowledge within the academy, unequal status for teaching and unequal access to 'voice' within the classroom. In this atmosphere where working-class students feel they do not belong (McGivney, 1990) and where they may want to resist full engagement with their study in order to maintain their identity (Archer et al., 2003), who speaks up and who is silent is a significant issue. If lecturers do not examine classroom–laboratory interactions, it is likely that it is those students whose experience of the HE habitus is limited who will continue to be disadvantaged. This suggests that it is not enough to encourage student engagement in the classroom or in individual sessions, for a student voice is constructed by 'selection, interpretation and . . . social process through available discourses' (Burke, 2002, p. 58). In other words, greater attention needs to be paid to who speaks and who is able to engage. Few HE professional teaching courses examine issues of widening participation or prior student experience, which is a further indication that we have some way to go to address the needs of new learners. As Frand (2000) points out:

> The outlook of those we teach has changed, and thus the way in which we teach must change. The world in which we all live has changed, and thus the content we teach must change. The industrial age has become the information age, and thus the way we organise our institutions must change as must the meaning we attach to the terms 'student', 'teacher' and 'alumni'. (p. 24)

Quality assurance in learning and teaching at HE level is determined in Britain by the Quality Assurance Agency. However, their discourse of quality has paid scant attention to the widening participation agenda. Until the last round of subject review the issue of student success was not really examined and even now the question of trajectory and value-added is seldom really acknowledged. To take one example, a major theme of the quality regime is transparency for the student, which in itself is obviously a 'good idea'. However, transparency for lecturing staff and quality assurance professionals is not necessarily the same as for students, particularly students who do not have the language and discourses of HE. Burke (2002) uses the example of the 'checksheet', often regarded as good practice in learning and teaching:

> The checksheet may appear to be transparent to the teacher who has written it; however her/his meanings may be misinterpreted by the students reading it. This throws the notion of transparency into question. (p. 67)

Equally worrying, Maxwell (1996) points out developments in the Open College Network, which had been a flexible and enabling qualifications framework for students returning to study, but has now become a bureaucratic system which does not really take account of student need. As Howard points out; 'lifelong learning begins to focus on people ... rather than systems...' (Howard, 2002). However, the measurement of quality is determined by institutions that in some senses have found ways as any bureaucracy does to self-perpetuate, reproducing themselves and knowledge about HE to ensure their own survival (Gerth and Wright Mills, 1946).

The poor cousin – vocational HE

Recently, new sites of learning for HE are being developed. HE learning in the twenty-first century will not be only be focused on HE institutions and may well be delivered in the workplace (DfES, 2003). However, even in work-related learning, access is unequally divided, '. . . the main beneficiaries of spending on workplace vocational education and training being the . . . more highly skilled and those working in large organisations' (Taylor and Cameron, 2002, p. 23). Britain has a much less developed workforce development policy framework than countries such as Germany and France. One clear reason for this is the low status of vocational education and training in the UK. This is a major drawback for developing the widening participation agenda in HE as vocational HE is particularly considered to be low-status teaching. The value of vocational learning needs to be established, especially in the light of the history of higher education in Britain. In reality, HE has always been vocational, first as a training ground for clerics; then during the nineteenth century came the great growth of vocational HE as new professions developed training for doctors and lawyers, and engineers were admitted to the academy.

Increasingly, students are becoming instrumental and feel the need for vocational outcomes. This is not only in relation to directly vocational courses and not only in institutions that have focused on vocational learning. In Ahier et al. (2003) a study on students and citizenship found that students were concerned about what a university degree could buy you. One of their interviewees, a working-class young man at Cambridge University, and the first in his family to go to university put it this way:

> I've really worked really hard so I think that should be rewarded in some way. You know, a certain recognition through the status of career, salary perhaps. Obviously it's difficult because you always come back to the Cambridge thing, you know, and certainly I think you earn the right here to be respected, well, because of the place, because obviously you've come to Cambridge, you know, obviously the degree is highly revered, therefore you earn the right to be respected within the workplace. (Kelvin, in Ahier, Beck and Moore, 2003, p. 120)

Kelvin is concerned about the quality of future career but in this sense he is relying on the status of the institution itself rather than the subject he has studied. This perspective is equally important in the debate about vocationalism but is seldom discussed, making vocational HE to be seen as a lesser provision, no longer including training for doctors and engineers, or including getting a degree from Cambridge, but now centred on a perspective of skill development, largely offered in HE in further education. Negative attitudes to vocational education are deep-rooted in British society. Archer et al. (2003) eloquently sum up the difficulties inherent in the vocation/academic divide in the UK:

> Resistance to vocational education, or to some forms of vocational education, has come from a number of different directions [and goes back before the nineteenth century], including academics on the left of the political spectrum, New Right traditionalists and aspects of the media. (p. 141)

The Quality Assurance Agency has raised questions of the quality of vocational HE, particularly the programmes offered in further education colleges and in the workplace. While it is likely that some of these concerns are valid, there are also questions about to what extent there is an understanding of vocational HE learning.

Developing excellence in learning and teaching in this area needs further work to ensure we have a true picture of this vital part of the widening participation agenda. The British Government's emphasis on developing foundation degrees as the new intermediary HE level qualification will flounder if the status of vocational education is not addressed. All learning at HE level, but perhaps especially vocational HE, must not be focused on skill development only, but needs to take account of a broader, lifelong learning context. As Field (2000) suggests about lifelong learning:

> The first and most obvious is that learning how to learn becomes a priority. Unambiguously, the focus must be on learning rather than teaching, and this is not as simple as it sounds . . . This means moving away from teaching on the basis of simple precepts (what works) towards a more context-dependent, responsive and above all active approach to learner support . . . The challenge is how to design a curriculum which enables young people to develop the confidence and skills to become effective learners through – out their lives. (p. 136)

Developing this curriculum will require a wider social involvement. As the ACU (2001) points out, this task cannot be undertaken by academics themselves:

> We need others to engage with us in the business of planning and monitoring higher education. We need to encourage others, especially employers, to help us with our broad agenda by engaging with us in addressing issues such as: how to strike a balance between narrow, vocationally-focused courses and broad programmes designed to prepare students for future life? (p. 13)

All these different factors; the context of compulsory education, the identities and experiences of the 'new' students, the status of learning and teaching and the role of particular types of institutions which engage in HE provision, suggest that developing excellence in learning and teaching for social inclusion in HE is extremely complex. Student success in this context cannot be achieved without a broader social engagement in the development of learning, teaching and curricula.

What way forward?

I began the chapter highlighting two perspectives on widening participation to and through HE, one that focused on additional support and one that argued for a transformation of HE culture and engagement with students. I have argued that the experience of students from poorer backgrounds in school, in their communities and in society suggests that there may well be a need for HE to provide more individually tailored learning programmes, but I would also argue that HE will need to transform itself to be more engaged with the changing society, young people and the needs of the twenty-first century. As Castells (1996) observes, in the network society in which we now live, connections are no longer simply linear and are more unequally distributed. I have also suggested that HE cannot and should not be expected to deliver widening participation by itself. All of the education system needs to engage with its class-ridden past and examine new ways of engaging with diverse learners.

As well as education tackling discrimination within its institutions and practices, widening participation, and teaching and learning practices that create student success have to include a wide range of partners. There are examples of good practice both in the UK and abroad. Schemes such as the Pathways to College Network that specifically work with communities to ensure social equity for students highlight the way forward. This programme, offered in the United States, works with local communities as advocates for their young people.

> It) . . . emphasises the involvement of parents and families and engagement of community leaders in advocacy efforts to improve and

support opportunities for under-represented youth. Work in this area is based on the premise that successful pathways to college are the shared responsibility of students, parents, families, schools and community and business leaders. (Coles and Roth, 2002, p. 89)

Working in this way means that communities are able to point out where 'taken for granted' practices discriminate against students from backgrounds where HE is not part of their family experience.

There are also, increasingly, examples of new pedagogies, such as 'just in time' teaching (jitt.org), which include using learning materials as students need them and when they will make sense. This is increasingly used in vocational areas of HE such as engineering, as well as in the sciences such as physics. This is an example of what Barnet (1997) suggests should be a key function of the HE in the twenty-first century, drawing more on performative epistemologies rather than the previously sacrosanct contemplative epistemologies. As Frand (2000) states:

> This vision challenges our institutions not only to look at new ways of doing what we have always done but also to look at new things. Students with an information-age mindset expect education to emphasise the learning process more than a canon of knowledge. They want to be part of learning communities, with hubs and spokes of learners, rejecting the broadcast paradigm of television (or the notetaker in a lecture hall). Our institutions need to expand their primary focus from the internal, on-campus, temporal experience to include the external, global, lifelong experience (p. 24)

This is a transformative approach because it is working with the students' immediate needs rather than focusing on the curriculum and its needs.

More radical solutions and theories such as participatory learning and action (Stuart, 2002; Taylor, 2003) which facilitate engagement with communities and challenge discrimination in the classroom are also increasing in popularity. Many of these pedagogies grew out of development programmes in the South and have now been adopted by people working in the northern hemisphere. Participatory methods are rooted in enabling people to take control of their own lives. The process is about giving people the confidence to explore, to challenge and to develop theories for themselves. These are some of the key elements of a higher-level education. Rather than talking at students, this approach involves them in self- and group-discovery with the teacher/lecturer as facilitator rather than being the gatekeeper of knowledge:

> . . . doing participation . . . means dealing with relationships; understanding human behaviour; facilitating the reduction of social barriers to working together; and building capacity for people to deal with complex, dynamic and often conflicting group or community processes. (Hagman and Almekinders et al., 2003, p. 21)

This approach will encompass deficiencies in the student's learning but will also engage the student's knowledge which, as Frand (2000) argues, may not be known by the lecturer. Working in this way will tackle some of the difficult issues raised in this chapter such as questions of educational and social disadvantage, as well as questions of student identity and institutional habitus. This is also a route into applied ethical research. Again many of these techniques are used in the field of development across the Arts, social and hard sciences. Good teaching and learning in HE does require links into appropriate research. These techniques also provide an excellent methodology for partnership and work with communities, families, schools and other social agencies. While these pedagogies do go some way to resolving some of the debates about widening participation, teaching and learning raised in this chapter, there are still some questions that require resolving in Britain, such as the status of vocational HE and the status of widening participation work itself. These issues have a knock-on impact on institutions that are involved in this work. Widening participation to and through HE remains part of a political campaign for social justice and social inclusion. Students who are currently being encouraged to take on further study in Britain through such schemes as Aimhigher (HEFCE, 2004), which seek to raise aspirations and attainment towards HE, need to feel confident that the learning and teaching environment for their HE level study will be developed with their experience and needs in mind. If this is not so, then as Archer et al. (2003) point out, 'for individual working-class students ... participation may entail considerable social and psychic burdens, and 'failure' (or withdrawal) may have serious personal, social and/or economic implications for . . . students' (p. 199). The price of social inclusion is still high for all concerned.

References

Ahier, J., Beck, J. and Moore M. (2003) *Graduate Citizens? Issues of Citizenship and Higher Education*. London: Routledge.

Apple, M. (1990) *Ideology and Curriculum*. London: Routledge.

Archer, L., Hutchings M. and Ross M. (2003) *Higher Education and Social Class*. London: Routledge Falmer.

Association of Commonwealth Universities (ACU) (2001) *Engagement as a Core Value for the University*. London: ACU.

Barnet, R. (1997) *Towards a Higher Education for a New Century*. London: Institute of Education.

Beck, U. (1992) *The Risk Society Towards a New Modernity*. London: Sage.

Bourdieu, P. (1984) *Distinction: a Social Critique of the Judgement of Taste*. London: Routledge.

Bowl, M. (2003) *Non-Traditional Entrants to Higher Education: 'They talk about people like me'*. Stoke on Trent: Trentham Books.

Brown, R. and Piatt, W. (2001) *Funding Widening Participation in Higher Education: A Discussion Paper*. London: CIHE.

Burke, P. (2002) *Accessing Education Effectively Widening Participation*. Stoke on Trent: Trentham Books.

Bynner, J. and Joshi, H. (2002) 'Equality and Opportunity in

Education: Evidence from the 1958 and 1970 birth cohort studies', *Oxford Review of Education*, Vol. 28, No 4, pp. 405–26.

Castells, M. (1996) *The Rise of the Network Society*. Oxford: Blackwell.

Coles, A. and Roth, D. M. (2002) Pathways to College Networks: Collaborating nationally to improve college access and success for under represented students in the US. In Thomas L., Cooper, M. and Quinn, J. *Collaboration to Widen Participation in Higher Education*. Stoke on Trent: Trentham Books.

Delors, J. (1997) *International Commission on Education for the 21st Century*. Paris: UNESCO.

Denholm, J. and Macleod D. (2003) *Prospects for Growth: A literature review*. London: Learning and Skills Development Agency.

Dearing, R. (1997) *Higher Education and the Learning Society*. London: National Committee of Inquiry into Higher Education.

DfES (2003) *The Future of Higher Education*. January, 2003.

Field, J. (2000) *Lifelong Learning and the New Educational Order*. Stoke on Trent: Trentham Books.

Fielding, M. (ed.) (2001) *Taking Education Really Seriously: Four Years Hard Labour*. London: Routledge Falmer

Frand, J. L. (2000) 'The Information-age Mindset Changes in Students and Implications for Higher Education', *Educause Review*, September/October 2000, pp. 15–24.

Gerth, H. and Wright Mills, C. (1946) *From Max Weber*. New York: Oxford University Press.

Giddens, A. (1991) *Modernity and Self-Identity: Self and society in the late modern age*. Cambridge: Polity Press.

Hagmann, J. and Almekinders, C. (2003) Developing 'Soft Skills' in Higher Education. In Taylor, P. (2003), *Learning and Teaching Participation*. London: International Institute for Environment and

Development.

HEFCE (2004) *Aimhigher: Guidance notes for integration*, 2004/08.

Howard, A. (2002) Introduction in S. Taylor and H. Cameron (eds) (2002). *Attracting New Learners: International evidence andpPractice*. London: LSDA.

Ivanic, R. (1993) *The Discoursal Construction of Writer Identity: An investigation of eight mature students*. Lancaster University, unpublished Ph.D. thesis.

Johnston, R. (2003) 'Widening Participation; Higher education and the risk society', *Journal of Access Policy and Practice*, Vol.1, No 1, Autumn 2003.

jitt.org (2004) http://websphysics.iupui.edu/jitt/jitt.html

Lawrence, J. (2002) Academics and the First-year Students; Collaborating to access success in an unfamiliar university culture. In: L. Thomas, M. Cooper and J. Quinn (2002) (eds), *Collaboration to Widen Participation in Higher Education*. Stoke on Trent: Trentham Books.

Layer, G., Stuart, M. and Srivastava, A. (2003) *Student Success in Higher Education*. Bradford: (Action on Access) University of Bradford.

McGivney, V. (1990) *Education's for Other People*. Leicester: NIACE.

McNicols, S. (2004) 'Widening Participation and Policy Debates – Comparing the 20 and 21st Centuries', *Journal of Access Policy and Practice*, Vol. 1, No 2, Spring 2004.

Massey, D. and Jess, P, (1995) (eds) *A Place in the World? Places, cultures and globalisation*. Milton Keynes: Open University Press.

Maxwell, B. (1996) 'Open College Networks; Are they still for Adult Learners?' *Adults Learning*, January 1996, pp. 111–12.

Meadows, P. (2001) *Young Men on the Margins of Work: An overview*. Report, Joseph Rowntree Foundation.

Miles, S. (2000) *Youth Lifestyles in a Changing World.* Milton Keynes: Open University Press.

Office of National Statistics (2001) *Social Trends*, Vol. 31. London: The Stationery Office.

Osborne, M, (2003) 'Policy and practice in widening participation: a six country comparative study of access as flexibility', *International Journal of Lifelong Education*, Vol. 22, No 1, pp. 43–59.

Parry, G. and Thompson, A. (2002) *Closer by Degrees: The past, present and future of higher education in further education colleges.* London: Learning and Skills Development Agency.

Rhodes, C., Bill, K., Biscomb, K. and Nevil, A. (2002) Widening participation in higher education: support at the further education/higher education interface and its impact on the transition and progression of advanced GNVQs – a research report. *Journal of Vocational Education and Training*, Vol. 54, No 1, pp. 133–45.

Rustin, M. (2000) The Biographical Turn. In Chamberlayne, P., Bornat, J. and Wengaraf, T. (2000), *The Turn to Biographical Methods in the Social Sciences.* London: Routledge.

Steedman, H. (2001) *Learning for Work: Notes on presentation at the Attracting New Learners Seminar*, 27–28 June 2001, Learning and Skills Development Agency.

Stuart, M. (1999) Writing, the Self and the Social Process. In C. Hunt and F. Sampson, *The Self on the Page; Theory and practice of creative writing in personal development.* London: Jessica Kingsley.

Stuart, M. (2002) *Collaborating for Change: Managing widening participation in further and higher education.* Leicester: NIACE.

Taylor, P. (2003) *Learning and Teaching Participation.* London: International Institute for Environment and Development.

Taylor, S. and Cameron, H. (eds) (2002) *Attracting New Learner: International evidence and practice.* London: LSDA.

Tett, L. (2000) I'm Working Class and I'm Proud Of It; Gendered experiences of non-traditional participants', *HE Gender and Education*, Vol. 12, No 2, pp. 183–94.

The Times Higher Education Supplement (THES) (2004a) Access Universities with Empty Seats Pay the Price in HEFCE Cuts, 5 March, p. 1.

The Times Higher Education Supplement (THES) (2004b) Cut-price Policy Bites, 5 March, p. 13.

The Times Higher Education Supplement (THES) (2004c) Graduate Glut Claims Rubbished, 30 April, p. 2.

Thomson, P. (2002) *Schooling and the Rustbelt Kids Making the Difference in Changing Times*. Stoke on Trent: Trentham Books.

Watson, D. (2002) 'Can We Do it All? Tensions in the Mission and Structure of UK Higher Education', *Higher Education Quarterly*, Vol. 56, No 2, pp. 143–55.

Chapter 8

Access where? Access to what? Towards a comprehensive assessment

Alexander C. McCormick

In this paper I examine current evidence on the successes and challenges of the long-standing 'access' agenda in the United States, with particular attention to how we fall short of the meritocratic ideal. I argue for a comprehensive assessment of access that looks beyond simple measures of participation, enquiring into the types of institutions attended (access *where*) and the attendant prospects for degree completion (access *to what*). Although discussions of access consider many demographic sub-groups of concern – racial-ethnic minorities, women, and students from low socio-economic (SES) backgrounds, this paper concentrates primarily on the last group. I conclude with a brief discussion of recent trends in public discourse regarding higher education, and the threat this may pose to the access agenda.

The United States has a long tradition of concern with extending the benefits of higher education to a wider segment of its population. The Agricultural College Act of 1862, more commonly known as the Morrill Act (after Senator Justin Smith Morrill of Vermont), established land-grant colleges to increase the diffusion of scientific knowledge and its practical application in agriculture and industry, as well as 'to promote the liberal and practical education of the industrial classes'. The second Morrill Act (1890) extended access to higher education to African-Americans, establishing what would later come to be known as historically Black colleges and universities. The Servicemen's Readjustment Act of 1944 (commonly known as the GI Bill of Rights, after the colloquial term for American soldiers in World War II) provided funding to enable returning servicemen to pursue higher education, driving a major expansion of higher education that had dramatic consequences for American society. The National Defense Education Act (1958) and the Higher Education Act of 1965 established federal financial assistance for students, extending access to higher education to millions of students. In 1960, California established its Master Plan for Higher Education, establishing distinct segments within its public higher education system, with distinct missions and recognising distinct educational needs of different segments of the student population. While contemporary analysts may look back on the Master Plan and see elitism or structural inequity, it embodied remarkable optimism – founded on meritocratic ideals, to be sure – in its attempt to provide a route to higher education for virtually all high school graduates in the State.

A remarkable feature of higher education in the United States is its relative openness: no barriers to initial entry are imposed by a student's programme of secondary education (though particular institutions may specify recommended or required courses); many institutions offer open admission contingent only upon a student's 'ability to benefit;' students can enrol on a part-time basis, or take classes at night and on weekends, to accommodate their other commitments and obligations; students can interrupt their education and resume their studies after many years; and students can enrol at several institutions, either simultaneously or serially, and consolidate these discrete experiences into a single degree. Even incarceration does not preclude work toward a college degree. The pursuit and continuation of higher education is virtually never foreclosed, and indeed every year we see press accounts of octogenarians completing their college degree. This openness accounts, at least in part, for the relatively weak correspondence between American students' academic experiences and their educational aspirations: students can maintain lofty ambitions entirely apart from their academic preparation and their enrolment activity.

This openness manifests itself in the national data on participation. First, consider the immediate transition from high school to college: according to the 2001 Current Population Survey, 62 per cent of new high school graduates were enrolled in college in October of that year. Enrolment rates varied with respect to family income and race-ethnicity, however: from 44 per cent among low-income to 80 per cent among high-income families; 64 per cent among whites; 55 per cent among African-Americans; and 52 per cent among Latinos (US Department of Education, 2002). Because this fails to capture enrolment by older students – another dimension of the openness described above – consider the age distribution of undergraduates: in 1999–2000, about one-third of students at baccalaureate-level[1] institutions and more than half of those at community colleges were age 24 or older (the percentages for age 30 or older were 16 and 36 per cent, respectively) (Horn et al., 2002). Finally, consider evidence of the 'swirl' of students among institutions, as revealed in a recent analysis of college transcripts spanning eight years after high school: among a cohort of 1992 high school seniors who continued their education and had earned more than 10 credits, 57 per cent enrolled at more than one institution, as did 59 per cent of those who completed a bachelor's degree (Adelman et al., 2003).

This is not to say, however, that all aspirants can readily enact their dreams, nor does it imply that differences in the specific nature of postsecondary participation are unimportant. Higher education in the USA is highly stratified, with a small number of institutions widely recognised as 'elite' or 'medallion' schools – most but not all private institutions – where undergraduate admission is highly competitive, where retention and graduation rates are very high, and which confer upon their graduates a broad range of social and economic benefits. At the other end of the status continuum are open-access institutions: commuter campuses and community colleges, where costs are considerably lower, as are the odds of bachelor's degree completion (reflecting, in part, many factors that are beyond the control or influence of the institutions). Between these extremes resides a large and diverse group of institutions, both public and private, from exclusively undergraduate colleges to doctorate-granting universities, which produce the majority of the nation's bachelor's degree graduates. Although access to higher education has been a long-standing policy concern in the USA, a thorough assessment of access should consider more than simple entry into the system. An equally important question to ask is, 'access *where?*' (Karabel and Astin, 1975; Carnevale and Rose, 2003; Astin and Oseguera, 2004). Similarly, a comprehensive analysis of access also requires going beyond questions of simple entry to consider persistence and degree completion, in other words, 'access *to what?*' (The latter question has recently been expanded to include important questions of student learning, for which credit accumulation and degree completion are imperfect proxies. For example, see Gumport and Zemsky, 2003).

Access *where?*

Expanding the access question to 'access where?' shifts attention to the matching of students to institutions, which involves two choice processes: students' choice of institutions, and in a selective admissions context, institutions' choice of students. The matching of students to institutions represents the complex interplay of many factors, such as: elementary and secondary educational opportunities; information acquisition by students and parents about college opportunities, preparatory courses, course sequences, financial aid, and application processes; academic achievement; preparation for and performance on standardized tests; completion of college applications; and evaluation of applications by college personnel. Although education in the United States is rationalised as fundamentally meritocratic, in which opportunity is extended on the basis of demonstrated ability and promise rather than family background, each of these stages is vulnerable to intrusion or interference by factors other than individual merit. Although a full treatment of all these factors is beyond the scope of this paper, in the following pages I will expand on important concerns relating the matching of students to institutions to issues of access and social inclusion.

The sociological critique of the meritocratic account of educational opportunity and social mobility can be distilled as follows: social-structural arrangements systematically restrict mobility by low-SES and minority students, but the rhetoric of meritocracy transforms these obstacles into instances of individual failure. In a richly detailed case study of college search and college choice by six high-SES and six low-SES students of like gender, race, and academic records attending four high schools with different formal and informal resources to assist students in the search/choice process, Patricia McDonough documents the complex interplay of social class, family, peer group, and school influences (McDonough, 1997). In her concluding chapter, McDonough observes how this reality measures up to the assumptions of meritocracy:

> Not all college-bound students face equal choices if they start out with different family and school resources that enable or constrain their educational and occupational mobility possibilities. These differential resources contribute to the persistence and reproduction of a social-class-based stratified system of postsecondary opportunity that thwarts meritocratic ideals. (p. 150)

Yet the merit principle is a powerful force in American educational ideology, and it has figured prominently in recent debates in US higher education, as will be discussed at the end of this paper.

In the US educational system, selectivity of undergraduate admissions is, not surprisingly, highly correlated with institutional prestige: the most desirable institutions turn away many more students than they accept, and a substantial share of those rejected are highly qualified. These institutions also have very high yield rates, meaning the proportion of accepted students who choose to accept the offer of admission and enrol. These institutions enrol a very small share of students in US higher education. But in light of their national (and often international) prominence as well as their economic and cultural importance, it is reasonable to investigate the successes and failures of access at selective colleges and universities. Put another way, it would be deeply troubling if we were to find that academically talented low-income or minority students enjoy access to higher education, but not to our most prestigious institutions.[2]

Recent analyses have documented an inverse relationship between selectivity and the proportion of low-SES students enrolled. Carnevale and Rose analysed the enrolment histories of two high school graduating cohorts a decade apart, assigning baccalaureate-granting colleges and universities attended to one of four selectivity 'tiers' according to college guide ratings, with community colleges constituting a fifth group (Carnevale and Rose, 2003). For the more recent cohort (1992 high school graduates), they found that students from the bottom half of the SES distribution accounted for only nine per cent of students attending top-tier schools. The corresponding percentages in the next three tiers were 25, 29, and 37, respectively, and 51 per cent at community colleges. Students from the top SES quartile, by contrast, represented about three-quarters of the students attending top-tier schools.

An important methodological issue needs to be considered here. Admissions selectivity is most often operationalised by the average standardised college admission test score (SAT or ACT) for an institution's entering class, and it is one component of the college guide selectivity classification used in this study. It is well known that scores on these tests are positively correlated with the socioeconomic background of the test-taker (Camara and Schmidt, 1999). Thus it should not be surprising to find an over-representation of high-SES students at selective schools when 'selectivity' is measured by the average scores of entering students. The relationship between SES and test scores is not perfect, however, and there are exceptions in both directions: low-SES students with high scores, and high-SES students with low scores. Other analyses of SES differences in college attendance have shown that high-SES students are more able than their low-SES counterparts to overcome a low score in gaining admission to selective colleges and universities.

In a simple demonstration of the how meritocratic ideals break down that complements McDonough's work, Carnevale and Rose investigated the influence of secondary school context and resources on selective college enrolment by examining low-SES students from low- and high-income schools (where the income context of a school was operationalised by the proportion of students eligible to receive subsidised lunch). They found that relative to their counterparts at low-income schools, low-SES students at high-income schools performed better on tests of cognitive ability; were more likely to take college entrance examinations (64 per cent versus 37 percent); performed better on those exams (40 per cent versus 19 per cent scoring an SAT-equivalent of 1,000 or better); and of those who enrolled at a four-year institution, they were more likely to attend one in the top two tiers of selectivity (30 per cent versus 16 per cent).

This brings us to a critical factor in considering access to top institutions, one that is fundamental to meritocratic ideology: quality of academic preparation. Studying the same cohort of 1992 high school seniors, Berkner and Chavez (1997) estimated students' 'college qualification' using a range of measures: performance on a cognitive ability test administered as part of the longitudinal study; high school grades; high school class rank; standardised college admission test scores; and a measure of the academic rigour of the high school curriculum. This analysis found substantial differences in college qualification relative to family income, parents' education, and race-ethnicity. For example, 53 per cent of low-income students were judged to be qualified for college admission, including 21 per cent who were highly or very highly qualified, compared with 86 per cent qualified among high-income students and 56 per cent at least highly qualified (Berkner and Chavez, 1997; US Department of Education, 1998). Among qualified students, the likelihood of college enrolment was positively related to family income. But importantly, among college-qualified students *who took a college entrance exam and applied for admission,* low- and middle-income students enrolled at comparable rates (82 per cent enrolling at a baccalaureate institutions, and 11–13 per cent enrolling at a two-year college). The college acceptance and enrolment advantage for high-income students persisted, though it was much attenuated after controlling for application behaviors. In a simple multivariate analysis of four-year college enrolment controlling for background characteristics (family income, race-ethnicity, and parents' education), college qualification, and application behaviors, however, both income and parents' education showed independent effects, while race-ethnicity did not.

In an important and influential study, Clifford Adelman used high school transcript data from another longitudinal high school cohort study (1982 high school seniors) to devise a highly nuanced measure of the curricular rigour of students' high school preparation, a 40-point scale which he termed 'academic intensity' (Adelman, 1999). Next, he combined this measure with cognitive ability test scores and a measure of high school achievement into a broad index of 'academic resources,' which was moderately correlated with socioeconomic status (r = 0.37). Adelman examined the correspondence between this variable and bachelor's degree completion for all students and also within SES quintiles. The analysis shows a systematic linear relationship between academic resources and bachelor's degree completion within SES quintiles: fully 62 per cent of low-SES students in the top quintile of academic resources completed a bachelor's degree, exceeding, for example, the completion rate for high-SES students in the bottom three academic resources quintiles (13 to 51 per cent). Among the most advantaged group, high-SES students in the top academic resources quintile, 86 per cent completed the degree.

Taken together, these findings reinforce an observation by Carnevale and Rose from their own analysis of college qualification of low-SES students:

> The conventional view that academic preparation is a monolithic barrier to access and choice among low-SES students is greatly overstated and an unnecessary barrier to policies that can have immediate effects. There are large numbers of students from families with low income and low levels of parental education who are academically prepared for bachelor's degree attainment, even in the most selective colleges. Their numbers are far larger than those who currently attend. (p. 38)

The authors conclude from their analysis that high-ability low-SES students, 31 per cent of whom did not continue their education, 'are the low hanging fruit in any policy strategy to increase SES diversity in four-year colleges, including selective colleges' (p. 39).

Finally, there is some new evidence that the SES composition of student bodies at the most selective colleges and universities has been changing. Astin and Oseguera (2004) analysed time series data from the Cooperative Institutional Research Program (CIRP) surveys of first-year students. These data showed a 16-year trend of increasing over-representation of students from high-income families (top quartile of those in the sample) at the most selective schools, culminating at 55 per cent in 2000; declines in the proportion of middle-income students (middle quartiles), to 33 per cent in 2000; and the representation of low-income students staying relatively stable, and the lowest of the three, at 13 per cent. And while the distribution of parents' education changed dramatically over the period studied, the authors found evidence of an increasing concentration of first-generation college students in least selective institutions. Finally, in a comparison of multivariate linear probability models of enrollment at a highly selective institution between 1990 and 2000, they found evidence of continued independent impact of family background after controlling for ability and achievement characteristics, and an increase in the impact of family income.

Access *to what?*

Now let us consider the second phase of understanding college access: after students get in the door, what happens to them? Key markers of educational progress to consider are enrollment persistence and degree completion.

Retention and graduation rates are highest in the nation's most selective institutions; the graduation rate advantage holds even after statistically controlling for achievement characteristics of the student body (Bowen and Bok, 1998; Carnevale and Rose, 2003). Thus the access benefits for high-income students pay dividends beyond initial entry, as differential attrition rates manifest themselves. But for the remainder of this section, we will confine our attention to broader analyses of student success. The analysis that follows draws heavily on a study by Wei and Horn (2002) examining participation and outcomes for students participating in the federal government's largest need-based grant programme, the Pell Grant program, which primarily benefits middle- and low-income students. This study used longitudinal data for first-time college entrants who enrolled in 1995–96, and were followed up in 1998. Because the study covers only three years, the discussion will focus on the persistence findings. I should also note that although Pell Grant recipients were much more likely than others to have enrolled at private, for-profit, less-than-four-year institutions (about one in five did so), the summary below concentrates on those at community colleges and baccalaureate-level institutions (Wei and Horn, 2002).

Community colleges play a central role in extending access to higher education in the United States, particularly for low-income students because of their low cost of attendance and for working adults because of their convenience and flexible schedules. These institutions also extend access to under-prepared students, providing both high school completion and remedial/developmental courses to assist them in meeting the requirements for college-level academic work. Students working toward a bachelor's degree can complete their lower division coursework at a community college, then transfer to a baccalaureate-level institution to complete the degree. Finally, community colleges provide extensive offerings in vocational/technical training. In 1999–2000, 42 per cent of total enrolment in US postsecondary education was in public community colleges. (It is important to note that the extent and nature of community college systems varies considerably among the states.)

In 1995–96, about two out of five Pell Grant recipients were enrolled in community colleges. These students persisted at rates comparable to nonrecipients, though the rates are dismal in general (42 per cent 'remained enrolled at an institution of the same or higher level,' while 58 per cent stopped out, transferred down, or dropped out).[3] Among Pell Grant recipients in community colleges, about one in five indicated the intent to transfer to a four-year institution to complete a bachelor's degree, and the evidence suggests that a minority of this group will complete the degree. A subsequent analysis of the same data examining outcomes after five years found that half of those who had expressed transfer intentions did, in fact, transfer, as did one-quarter of those with associate's degree plans and one-fifth of those who did not specify a degree objective. Of those who transferred, about one-third had completed the degree and another 44 per cent were enrolled at a four-year institution (Hoachlander et al., 2003). (This study did not analyse Pell participants separately.) After a very thorough review of the evidence, Kevin Dougherty (1994) concludes that community college attendance hinders baccalaureate attainment.

Next, let us consider students attending baccalaureate-level colleges and universities, accounting for another two-fifths of Pell Grant recipients. Consistent with the findings of the previous section, selective institutions enrolled Pell Grant recipients at a lower rate than less selective institutions. But the general findings for students at four-year institutions are very encouraging: Pell Grant recipients persisted at rates equal to other students, even when controlling for entrance examination scores. The only exception was for students in the bottom quartile on entrance examination scores, where Pell recipients evidenced a *lower* dropout rate (Wei and Horn, 2002).

The Wei and Horn study concludes with a multivariate analysis of enrolment persistence that controlled for a range of student background characteristics and so-called risk factors, characteristics associated with increased risk of attrition.[4] Regrettably, because the analysis included students at all institution types, and measures of academic preparation and achievement were only available for students at four-year institutions, this important set of characteristics was excluded. The analysis found no effect for Pell participation, but independent positive effects for family income and parents' education, and negative effects for community college enrolment and for African-American students (among other effects not of direct concern for this paper). These intriguing findings beg further investigation with appropriate analytic refinements.

The individualist turn and its threat to the access agenda

Whereas in the 1960s and 70s discussions of the returns from higher education emphasised both individual and societal benefits (Bowen, 1978), in recent years the social benefit conception has faded far into the background. The individualist turn favors the development of policies and practices that are firmly rooted in a meritocratic vision of the educational system, and this threatens the maintenance and promotion of policies favouring increased access for low-income and minority students. Several developments reflect the individualist shift.

The rhetoric of challenges to affirmative action is based entirely in conceptions of individual benefit and simplistic notions of meritocracy. The claim is that majority students are victims of illegal discrimination when they are denied admission to selective colleges and universities in favour of ethnic minority students who have lower grades or test scores. Opponents of affirmative action assert that admission should be based exclusively on supposedly 'race-neutral' objective factors such as academic preparation and performance on entrance examinations. Arguments that student body diversity at the nation's top colleges and universities is a social good, both because it enriches the educational experience of all students and because it diversifies the population that will assume leadership positions in society, are rejected. Because meritocratic ideology is deeply embedded in American culture, the appeal to 'fairness' has won considerable support, the recent decision of the US Supreme Court in Gratz and Grutter notwithstanding.

As public high schools have cut their counselling staff, there has been a boom in private college admission counselling (McDonough et al., 1997). Naturally, the clientele for this expanding industry consists primarily of families from the middle and upper range of the income distribution (a segment that also disproportionately benefits from sophisticated college counselling at private secondary schools). Here again, the implicit message is that there is little public interest in assisting students of all backgrounds in the college admission process.

There has been a well-documented shift in the federal system of need-based financial aid. This system began explicitly to promote access for students who otherwise would have been unable to attend college. Grant programmes targeted low-income students, and federally guaranteed loans assisted middle-income students (Gladieux and King, 1999). As documented by Gladieux and King, the loan programmes expanded much faster than the grant programmes, such that grants now play a much smaller role in the financing of higher education for needy students. While the Pell Grant programme remains important, the purchasing power of a Pell Grant has fallen as the level of funding has failed to keep pace with rising college costs. Intended or not – the story arguably has more to do with the intricacies of the budget and appropriations process than with an explicit philosophical transformation – this change implies a shift from a social-benefit to an individual-benefit conception: since students will realise the economic benefits of higher education,[5] they should bear more responsibility for the cost. The notion that subsidising higher education for needy students is in the public interest, while still present in the interest rate subsidy of the loan programmes, has the lost prominence it had when grants played a central role.

Finally, there has been an explicit shift, at both state and federal levels, to link financial aid to academic achievement through merit scholarships (Heller and Marin, 2002). This transformation, which disproportionately benefits white students and students from middle- and upper-income families, represents a clear shift in favour of merit-ocratic ideology and its endorsement of earned advantage. Rewarding achievement does not inherently undermine the social-benefit conception. Indeed, the state merit programmes were predicated on a form of social benefit, the desire to induce talented students to remain in the State. But because their benefits fall disproportionately to already-advantaged groups, their effect is to divert attention – and resources – from other conceptions of social benefit.

Taken together with the evidence from the previous section regarding income-related imbalances in the nature of college access – that is, access *where* and access *to what* – this trend toward increasingly individualist conceptions of the benefits of higher education, undergirded by a powerful but myopic belief in meritocracy, poses a grave threat to America's historic commitment to access.

Notes

1   Throughout this paper, 'baccalaureate-level' and 'four-year' will be used interchangeably to denote colleges and universities that award at least a bachelor's degree.

2 I am intentionally – and perhaps awkwardly – avoiding the implication that admissions selectivity signifies educational quality. This is itself a matter of some debate and little evidence, and well beyond the scope of the present work.

3 Because of the wide range of student objectives and the many challenges confronted by their students, the interpretation of attrition rates is both murky and controversial. In this case, it should be noted that stopout is not uniformly a bad thing, and some of the students classified here as dropouts will almost certainly continue their education in the future.

4 Risk factors included: no high school diploma; delayed college entry; classification as financially independent for financial aid purposes; having dependents; single parenthood; part-time enrolment; and full-time employment.

5 This assumes successful completion; borrowers face repayment whether they graduate or not.

References

Adelman, C. (1999) *Answers in the Tool Box: Academic intensity, attendance patterns, and Bachelor's Degree attainment.* Washington, DC: US Department of Education, Office of Educational Research and Improvement.

Adelman, C., Daniel, B. and Berkovits, I. (2003) *Postsecondary Attainment, Attendance, Curriculum, and Performance: Selected results from the NELS:88/2000 Postsecondary Education Transcript Study (PETS), 2000.* Washington, DC: US Department of Education, National Center for Education Statistics.

Astin, A. W. and Oseguera, L. (2004) 'The Declining "Equity" of American Higher Education', *The Review of Higher Education*, Vol. 31, No 3, pp.321–41.

Berkner, L. K. and Chavez, L. (1997) *Access to Postsecondary Education for the 1992 High School Graduates.* Washington, DC: US Department of Education, National Center for Education Statistics.

Bowen, H. R. (1978) *Investment in Learning: The individual and social value of American higher education.* San Francisco: Jossey-Bass.

Bowen, W. G. and Bok, D. (1998) *The Shape of the River: Long-term consequences of considering race in college and university admissions.* Princeton: Princeton University Press.

Camara, W. J. and Schmidt, A. E. (1999) *Group Differences in Standardized Testing and Social Stratification.* New York: College Entrance Examination Board.

Carnevale, A. P. and Rose, S. J. (2003) *Socioeconomic Status, Race/Ethnicity, and Selective College Admissions.* New York: The Century Foundation.

Dougherty, K. J. (1994). *The Contradictory College: The conflicting origins, impacts, and futures of the Community College.* Albany: SUNY Press.

Gladieux, L. E. and King, J. E. (1999) The Federal Government and Higher Education. In P. G. Altbach, R. O. Berdahl and P. J. Gumport, *American Higher Education in the Twenty-first Century.* Baltimore: Johns Hopkins University Press.

Gumport, P. J. and Zemsky, R. (2003) 'Drawing New Maps for a Changing Enterprise', *Change,* Vol. 35, No 4.

Heller, D. E. and Marin, P. (eds) (2002) *Who Should We Help? The Negative Social Consequences of Merit Scholarships.* Cambridge: MA, The Civil Rights Project at Harvard University.

Hoachlander, G., Sikora, A. and Horn, L. (2003) *Community College Students: Goals, academic preparation, and outcomes.* Washington, DC: US. Department of Education, National Center for Education Statistics.

Horn, L., Peter, K., Rooney, K. and Malizio, A. (2002) *Profile of Undergraduates in US Postsecondary Institutions: 1999–2000.* Washington, DC: US Department of Education, National Center for Education Statistics.

Karabel, J. and Astin, A. W. (1975) 'Social Class, Academic Ability, and College "Quality"' in *Social Forces*, Vol. 53, No 3, pp. 381–98.

McDonough, P. M. (1997) *Choosing Colleges: How Social Class and Schools Structure Opportunity*. Albany: SUNY Press.

McDonough, P. M., Korn, J. and Yamasaki, E. (1997) 'Access, Equity, and the Privatization of College Counseling', *The Review of Higher Education*, Vol. 20, No 3, pp. 297–317.

US Department of Education (1998) *The Condition of Education 1998*. Washington, DC: US Government Printing Office.

US Department of Education (2002) *The Condition of Education 2002*. Washington, DC: US Government Printing Office.

Wei, C. C. and Horn, L. (2002) *Persistence and Attainment of Beginning Students with Pell Grants*. Washington, DC: U.S. Department of Education, National Center for Education Statistics.

Chapter 9

Closing the equity gap – is it sustainable?

Geoff Layer

This final short chapter is based on the discussions that took place at Bradford within the seminar and concludes with a model that helps to take planners and institutions forward. The seminar and the papers for the Bradford seminar, which have been further developed in this book, have sought to explore the issue of engagement in higher education from a range of political, social and economic perspectives as a means of seeking to shape national and international policy. The key issue throughout has been not simply looking at the drive towards wider participation but whether the systems that have been created are robust enough to make social inclusion within higher education (HE) sustainable. The challenge has always been to create a system that can deliver against the big picture and especially the distinction between being learner led rather than the existing dominant model of being provider led.

An interesting tension that was debated throughout the two days was whether systems can provide both 'equity' and 'excellence' as opposed to having to make a choice between the two. The strengths of the traditions of both 'equity' and 'excellence' within institutions tend to determine where individual organisations can position themselves within the market-place. The issue is whether the sector is an accumulation of the individual positions or whether the individual positions are determined once the goals and aspirations of the sector overall have been established. If left to market forces there is no clear undertaking that 'equity', 'excellence' or both will be sustainable.

Indeed the level of sustainability may vary according to particular courses of study.

There was a widespread recognition that different systems and countries are often difficult to compare without some data comparability issues arising. There was general agreement emerging from the seminar that despite the different collection systems and baselines etc., there was enough of a steer to be useful to unpick how systems were responding to similar questions.

There has been, and will continue to be, much debate about what we mean by participation. The key issue addressed in the seminar was the distinction between participation as measured by entry to HE courses and participation as defined by successful engagement with a programme of study. The tradition in most countries has been to measure participation by enrolment and not to then examine what happens to the learner, what they are studying or where and how they are engaging. Field, for example, in reporting on the Scottish position, where participation has already reached 50 per cent, was reporting that a considerable amount of this expansion had taken place outside universities in the further education sector. This was generally where students from the lower socio-economic groups were engaging and progression from such short cycle HE courses to particular universities was limited. This perspective, of course, assumes that the measurement of successful engagement in HE is engagement in universities on degree courses and that short cycle is a different form of experience.

The impact of student financial support arrangements was of particular interest to the English participants given the measures in the Higher Education Act 2004. The economic arguments about who pays and the levels of payment required were, as always, contested ground. However, the US experience of who actually prepares to pay, to save and to recognise the economic value of preparing for HE was demonstrating quite clearly that those from low-income families were least likely to save for HE. It was also clear that some of the changes in the US system were designed to support study in HE for all rather than a means of wealth redistribution (Baum). The financial support system was thus ever changing depending on the circumstances of that particular period of time. However, the financial system did not really distinguish how a student wished to study whereas the English proposals seek to regulate only the traditional student route of full-time study as opposed to part time (despite 42 per cent of undergraduates being part time).

As is always the case there is a shift taking place in the nature of higher education in most countries. While each country has its own agenda there are some common trends, particularly in respect of changing internal markets, target groups and political drivers. An example of this is around short cycle courses in terms of their development, public acceptance and the articulation arrangements, which even in the most planned environment did not appear to be overly transparent. This is a key challenge for the emerging Lifelong Networks (HEFCE, 2004) in England as without the progression framework being in place they will not succeed in being regarded as having parity of esteem among learners. The similar concept in the USA does not lead to the higher levels of progression expected or promised from two-year to four-year courses.

There was a general acceptance that in order to move forward there was a need to secure expansion to provide greater equity. This was because the concept of denying some individuals places in order to facilitate entry to others is problematic, as has been debated in the affirmative action policy issues in the USA and the subsequent intervention of the courts. The argument is that without expansion institutions have to socially engineer their enrolments to meet the equity agenda. Such moves create problems for the institutions, however transparent the policy, as they are admitting one student in preference to another using criteria that not everyone finds comfortable.

However, it is also clear that governments do not wish to finance that expansion and that they are increasingly looking to the beneficiaries themselves to fund it. Such a shift necessarily leads to a greater focus on the outcomes of HE and a shift to payment by results in the context of the beneficiary only being prepared to meet the outlay in return for a clear market advantage. Interestingly, a range of other stakeholders such as industry, employers and professional bodies are seeking a greater say in the nature of higher education at the very moment that it is moving from a publicly funded system to one that is more privately and individually funded.

As the systems continue to develop it is clear that a greater understanding of the issues is required in terms of addressing the nature of the product and seeking to match it to policy imperatives. This is evident in a number of strands of activity in terms of delivery and organisation as identifiable in college/university links, or in the preparation of students and staff for a different HE experience. This can be addressed in a number of ways, ranging from providing additionality for the under-represented groups to changing the nature of what we do (and have always done) to build from where this new group of learners is starting from both educationally and financially.

Watson developed the 'three Ps' as a conceptual model in Bradford. This focuses on the need to ensure:

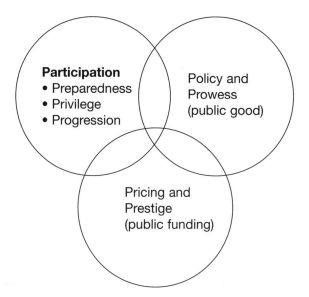

- **Preparedness** of the learner through ensuring their aspirations are raised, and that they are ready for the curriculum, the learning offered and the financial framework;
- **Pricing** that is sensitive to both institutional and target group need, recognising the nature of the market-place and captive markets as opposed to securing different participation;

- **Progression** that enables and facilitates student movement between and within institutions as the learner develops and changes;
- **Planning** that enables the sector to take account of the institutional and the learner need.

It is by addressing these issues slanted towards the policy imperative of equity that you can start to Close the Equity Gap and to make it sustainable.

References

Higher Education Statistics Agency (1997–2003) *Students in Higher Education Institutions*, Cheltenham: HESA.

Higher Education Funding Council for England (2004) *Lifelong Learning Networks*, June 2004. Bristol: HEFCE, 12/2004.

Higher Education Act 2004.

Index